The
Great Dane

An Owner's Guide To

A HAPPY HEALTHY PET

Howell Book House

Hungry Minds, Inc.
Best-Selling Books • Digital Downloads • e-Books • Answer Networks
e-Newsletters • Branded Web Sites • e-Learning
New York, NY • Cleveland, OH • Indianapolis, IN

Howell Book House
Hungry Minds, Inc.
909 Third Avenue
New York, NY 10022
www.hungryminds.com

For general information on Hungry Minds books in the U.S., please call our Consumer
Customer Service department at 800-762-2974. In Canada, please call (800) 667-1115. For
reseller information, including discounts and premium sales, please call our Reseller
Customer Service department at 800-434-3422.

Library of Congress Cataloging-in-Publication Data
Swedlow, Jill.
The great dane: an owner's guide to happy, healthy pet/by Jill Swedlow.
p.cm.
Includes bibliographical references
IISBN 0-87605-445-9
1. Great dane(Dogs)as pets. I. Title. II. Series.
SF429.G7584 1998, 2001   97-42056
636.73—dc20   CIP

Manufactured in the United States of America

10 9 8 7 6 5 4

Series Director: Kira Sexton
Book Design: Michele Laseau
Cover Design: Michael Freeland
Photography Editor: Richard Fox
Illustration: Jeff Yesh
Photography:
  Front and back cover photos supplied by Paulette Braun/Pets by Paulette
  Joan Balzarini: 96
  Mary Bloom: 54, 96, 136, 145
  Paulette Braun/Pets by Pauline: 30, 96
  Buckinghambill American Cocker Spaniels: 148
  Sian Cox: 134
  Dr. Ian Dunbar: 98, 101, 103, 111, 116–117, 122, 123, 127
  Howell Book House: 21
  Dan Lyons: 96
  Cathy Merrithew: 129
  Gayle Nelson: 20, 44
  Liz Palika: 133
  Don Petrulis: 22
  Cheryl Primeau: 16, 27, 52, 57 (top)
  Susan Rezy: 96–97
  Bob Schwartz: Title Page, 2–3, 18, 19, 28, 36, 48, 56, 58
  Judith Strom: 15, 34–35, 37, 41, 47, 68, 73, 96, 107, 110, 128, 130, 135, 137, 139, 140, 144,
  149, 150
  Jill Swedlow: 25, 26, 38
  Toni Tucker: 5, 8, 12, 60, 67, 83, 85
  Faith Uridel: 24, 57 (bottom)
  Jean Wentworth: 7, 9, 45, 59
Page creation by: Hungry Minds Indianapolis Production Department

Contents

part one

Welcome to the World of the Great Dane

1 What Is a Great Dane? 5

2 The Great Dane's Ancestry 18

3 The World According to the Great Dane 24

part two

Living with a Great Dane

4 Bringing Your Great Dane Home 36

5 Feeding Your Great Dane 47

6 Grooming Your Great Dane 54

7 Keeping Your Great Dane Healthy 60

part three

Enjoying Your Dog

8 Basic Training 98
by Ian Dunbar, Ph.D., MRCVS

9 Getting Active with Your Dog 128
by Bardi McLennan

10 Your Dog and Your Family 136
by Bardi McLennan

11 Your Dog and Your Community 144
by Bardi McLennan

part four

Beyond the Basics

12 Recommended Reading 151

13 Resources 155

Welcome
to the
World

of the

Great
Dane

External Features of the Great Dane

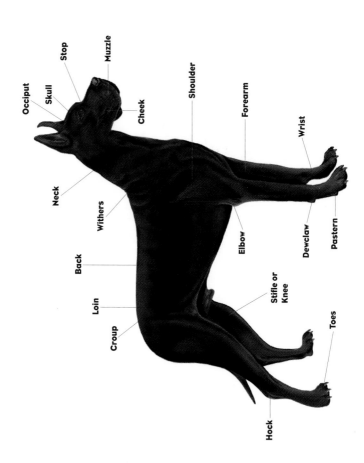

chapter 1

What

Is a

Great Dane?

The Great Dane is a giant breed that was first used as a fierce hunter and guardian of his master's property. The Great Dane of the past was far too aggressive to be considered a family pet. Today, after many years of careful breeding and adherence to the breed standard, the Great Dane is considered a wonderful and regal pet, the Gentle Giant, Apollo of dogs.

The Breed Standard

A novice cannot expect to fully understand the breed standard even if he or she has memorized it. Understanding the true meaning of this "blueprint" for a Great Dane takes a great deal of dedication and study. However, simply having some knowledge of what is considered to be the "perfect" Great Dane can greatly add to the novice's understanding of the breed.

The following excerpts and interpretations of the standard are provided for the novice who is about to purchase (or has just purchased) his or her first Great Dane. The definitions are an attempt to help you understand what is meant in layman's terms and is not intended as a full explanation of the standard language. Actual quotes from the standard are printed in italics, and explanations and comments are in regular type. To help you understand the Great Dane, this chapter accentuates features that are unique to the breed. For a copy of the complete AKC standard for the Great Dane, write to the American Kennel Club, 5580 Centerview Dr., Raleigh, NC 27690-0643.

The Great Dane Standard
GENERAL APPEARANCE

The Great Dane combines, in its regal appearance, dignity, strength and elegance with great size and a powerful, well-formed, smoothly muscled body. It is one of the giant working breeds, but is unique in that its general conformation must be so well balanced that it never appears clumsy, and shall move with a long reach and powerful drive. It is always a unit— the Apollo of dogs. A Great Dane must be spirited, courageous, never timid; always friendly and dependable. This physical and mental combination is the characteristic that gives the Great Dane the majesty possessed by no other breed. It is particularly true of this breed that there is an impression of great masculinity in dogs, as compared to an impression of femininity in bitches. Lack of true Dane breed type, as defined in this standard, is a serious fault.

This describes the overall appearance and desired temperament of the Great Dane. It should go without saying that a Great Dane is a VERY LARGE dog indeed. You should keep this in mind before choosing this breed.

As noted above, *A Great Dane must be spirited, courageous, never timid; always friendly and dependable.* These are important qualities in Great Danes because they were once extremely aggressive dogs. This is even more important to keep in mind when you pick out a puppy.

You do not want a puppy that shies away from you or slinks off to a corner to hide. A puppy that throws himself against your chest and tries to bite your chin is not the best choice either! A Great Dane should greet strangers in a friendly manner and have his tail wagging. An adult Great Dane should bark (or not) when he hears the doorbell, and then happily allow the visitor to enter once his owner has given the okay.

Great Danes are friendly, dependable and very large.

Size, Proportion, Substance

The male should appear more massive throughout than the bitch, with larger frame and heavier bone. In the ratio between length and height, the Great Dane should be square. In bitches, a somewhat longer body is permissible, providing she is well proportioned to her height. Coarseness or lack of substance is equally undesirable. The male shall not be less than 30 inches at the shoulders, but it is preferable that he be 32 inches or more, providing he is well proportioned to his height. The female shall not be less than 28 inches at the shoulders, but it is preferable that she be 30 inches or more, providing she is well proportioned to her height. Danes under minimum height must be disqualified.

This description simply means that a Great Dane should not resemble a Mastiff or a Greyhound. Males should look distinctly more masculine and taller than bitches. Substance means that the Great Dane has sufficiency of bone, frame size and muscle, giving him an impression of great size without too much bulk.

7

HEAD

The head shall be rectangular, long, distinguished, expressive, finely chiseled, especially below the eyes. Seen from the side, the Dane's forehead must be sharply set off from the bridge of the nose, (a strongly pronounced stop). The plane of the skull and the plane of the muzzle must be straight and parallel to one another. The skull plane under and to the inner point of the eye must slope without any bony protuberance in a smooth line to a full square jaw with a deep muzzle (fluttering lips are undesirable). The masculinity of the male is very pronounced in structural appearance of the head. The bitch's head is more delicately formed. Seen from the top, the skull should have parallel sides and the bridge of the nose should be as broad as possible. The cheek muscles should not be prominent. The length from the tip of the nose to the center of the stop should be equal to the length from the center of the stop to the rear of the slightly developed occiput. The head should be angular from all sides and should have flat planes with dimensions in proportion to the size of the Dane. Whiskers may be trimmed or left natural.

The Great Dane's head gives him a distinct and handsome appearance.

You should be able to identify the breed of a dog by his head. The Great Dane's head is important because it gives him a distinguished and regal appearance. It has been said that the head should have the appearance of two bricks of equal length arranged with one on top of the other. A short muzzle or round, wide skull tends to make a Great Dane resemble a Mastiff. On the other hand, when viewed from the side, a nose with a long, narrow bridge and no indent (or stop) along with a narrow back skull resembles the Greyhound.

EYES

Eyes shall be medium size, deep set, and dark, with a lively intelligent expression. The eyelids are almond-shaped and relatively tight, with well developed brows. Haws and Mongolian eyes are serious faults. In harlequins, the eyes should be dark; light colored eyes, eyes of different colors and walleyes are permitted but not desirable.

Whereas eye color has no impact on the health of the eye, the standard denotes a preference for a darker eye color. Haws (a protruding red membrane of the lower lid of the eye) can make the eyes more susceptible to eye infections which is, of course, quite unsightly. A Mongolian eye is one that has an exaggerated slant.

A Great Dane's uncropped ears usually hang like a hound's ears.

EARS

Ears shall be high set, medium in size and of moderate thickness, folded forward close to the cheek. The top line of the folded ear should be level with the skull. If cropped, the ear length is in proportion to the size of the head and the ears are carried uniformly erect.

Many people think that it is necessary to crop the Great Dane's ears in order for him to be shown. This has never been the case in the United States. However, because most of the Great Danes that are bred in America have cropped ears, breeders have not actively selected for the smaller, naturally high-set ear. If the Great Dane's ears are left uncropped, they tend to hang like a hound's ear; that is, low set and very large and droopy. Some people do not like this look. Cropping the ears helps prevent the development of hematomas (blood blisters in the ears) and makes the ears less prone to infection. The advantages and disadvantages of cropping are discussed in chapter 7.

NOSE

The nose shall be black, except in the blue Dane, where it is a dark blue-black. A black spotted nose is permitted on the harlequin; a pink colored nose is not desirable. A split nose is a disqualification.

A "split nose" is a nose with a cleft from the top to the bottom. It is a fairly difficult trait to find in Great Danes.

TEETH

Teeth shall be strong, well developed, clean and with full dentition. The incisors of the lower jaw touch very lightly the bottoms of the inner surface of the upper incisors (scissors bite). An undershot jaw is a very serious fault. Overshot or wry bites are serious faults. Even bites, misaligned or crowded incisors are minor faults.

Unless grossly malformed, an undershot (lower incisors protrude beyond the upper) or overshot (upper incisors protrude beyond the lower) mouth should have no effect on the health or well being of a Great Dane. Many dogs do not really chew their food, but tend to swallow it as is. However, in the show ring, a misaligned mouth would count against a Great Dane.

NECK, TOPLINE, BODY

The neck shall be firm, high set, well arched, long and muscular. From the nape, it should gradually broaden and flow smoothly into the withers. The neck underline should be clean. Withers shall slope smoothly into a short level back with a broad loin. The chest shall be broad, deep and well muscled. The forechest should be well developed without a pronounced sternum. The brisket extends to the elbow, with well-sprung ribs. The body underline should be tightly muscled with a well-defined tuck-up. The croup should be broad and very slightly sloping. The tail should be set high and smoothly into the croup, but not quite level with the back, a continuation of the spine. The tail should be broad at the base, tapering uniformly down to the hock joint. At rest, the tail should fall straight. When excited or running, it may curve slightly, but never above the level of the back. A ring or hooked tail is a serious fault. A docked tail is a disqualification.

The neck should be long and free of excess skin hanging under it. The length of the back should not be long (like a Dachshund's) or so short that the dog's feet are uncoordinated when he is active. The back should be level, with a slight downward slope that ends where the tail begins (the croup falls between where the downward slope ends and the tail). The back should not resemble a camel or be swayed like an old horse. When viewed from the side, the chest (or brisket) should be level with the elbows, and gently slope upward toward the hind legs and form a trim "waist." If there is no "waist" (tuck-up) either the dog is not anatomically correct or he's overweight. When viewed from the front, the chest should not be too narrow, nor should there be large bulging muscles on the shoulders like a Bulldog.

FOREQUARTERS

The forequarters, viewed from the side, shall be strong and muscular. The shoulder blade must be strong and sloping, forming, as near as possible, a right angle in its articulation with the upper arm. A line from the upper tip of the shoulder to the back of the elbow joint should be perpendicular. The ligaments and muscles holding the shoulder blade to the rib cage must be well developed, firm and securely attached to prevent loose shoulders. The shoulder blade and the upper arm should be the same length. The elbow should be one-half the distance from the withers to the ground. The strong pasterns should slope slightly. The feet should be round and compact with well-arched toes, neither toeing in, toeing out, nor rolling to the inside or outside. The nails should be short, strong and as dark as possible, except that they may be lighter in harlequins. Dewclaws may or may not be removed.

When viewed from the side, the shoulder should form a 90° angle to the front leg. There are three distinct portions of the foreleg: The shoulder blade begins at the base of the neck on the back and points forward where it articulates (touches) with the upper arm. The upper arm then angles back toward the rear of the dog and forms the elbow joint where it articulates with the lower foreleg. The foreleg should drop straight to the ground. The angles formed by the scapula and the humerus (upper arm) are what forms the angle of the forequarters. The degree of the angles here determines how far forward (reach) the dog can move his foreleg. The straighter the angle, the greater the stress that is put on the joints of the foreleg as it takes the weight of the dog while moving. Dogs with straighter joints may be more prone to lameness and have difficulty with movement.

When viewed from the front, the feet should not turn in or out. The feet should point straight ahead.

HINDQUARTERS

The hindquarters shall be strong, broad, muscular and well angulated, with well let down hocks. Seen from the rear, the hock joints appear to be perfectly straight, turned neither toward the inside nor toward the outside. The rear feet should be round and compact, with well-arched toes, neither toeing in nor out. The nails should be short, strong and as dark as possible, except they may be lighter in harlequins. Wolf claws are a serious fault.

Your Great Dane's rear legs provide him with a powerful gait.

Like the forequarters, the hindquarter should also form a 90° angle that is composed of the pelvis and the femur (upper thigh). The lower point of the thigh (some may refer to this as the rear "knee") is the stifle joint. The rear legs play an important role in what is called the "drive" in the gait. With proper forequarter and hindquarter angulation, the dog's drive is enhanced, and the more effortlessly the dog can move. Although it is important that a dog has the correct angulation, it is also important that the dog be balanced. This means that if the dog has less angulation in front, it's better that the rear angulation match so that the legs will not interfere with each other when in motion.

COAT

The coat shall be short, thick and clean with a smooth glossy appearance.

Color, Markings and Patterns

Brindle   *The base color shall be yellow gold and always brindled with strong black cross stripes in a chevron pattern. A black mask is preferred. Black should appear on the eye rims and eyebrows, and may appear on the ears and tail tip. The more intensive the base color and the more distinct and even the brindling, the more preferred will be the color. Too much or too little brindling are equally undesirable. White markings at the chest and toes, black-fronted, dirty colored brindles are not desirable.*

Fawn   *The color shall be yellow gold with a black mask. Black should appear on the eye rims and eyebrows, and may appear on the ears and tail tip. The deep yellow gold must always be given the preference. White markings at the chest and toes, black-fronted dirty colored fawns are not desirable.*

Blue   *The color shall be a pure steel blue. White markings at the chest and toes are not desirable.*

Black   *The color shall be a glossy black. White markings at the chest and toes are not desirable.*

Harlequin   Base color shall be pure white with black torn patches irregularly and well distributed over the entire body; a pure white neck is preferred. The black patches should never be large enough to give the appearance of a blanket, nor so small as to give a stippled or dappled effect. Eligible, but less desirable, are a few small gray patches, or a white base with single black hairs showing through, which tend to give a salt and pepper or dirty effect. Any variance in color or markings described above shall be faulted to the extent of the deviation. Any Great Dane that does not fall within the above color classifications must be disqualified.

For the family pet, color is basically unimportant. Just because certain coat colors may keep your Great Dane from competing in the show ring doesn't mean that he can't become a cherished family member. Note, however, that a white coat is associated with problems in the Great Dane. It is not uncommon for white dogs to be deaf and perhaps even blind. This can cause a host of training problems—unless you are prepared to actively manage such issues, you should avoid white dogs.

GAIT

The gait denotes strength and power with long, easy strides resulting in no tossing, rolling or bouncing of the topline or body. The backline shall appear level and parallel to the ground. The long reach should strike the ground below the nose while the head is carried forward. The powerful rear drive should be balanced to the reach. As speed increases, there is a natural tendency for the legs to converge toward the centerline of balance beneath the body. There should be no twisting in or out at the elbow or hock joints.

Just because a Great Dane is huge does not mean that he will be clumsy. An adult Dane that is romping should look sound and graceful. Even a young puppy should not be too clumsy. If you have a Dane that tends to fall down a lot or lose his balance, it's possible that he has a health problem. You should not hesitate to see a veterinarian under these circumstances.

TEMPERAMENT

The Great Dane must be spirited, courageous, always friendly and dependable, and never timid or aggressive.

Temperament is especially important in a breed the size of a Great Dane. A bite from this big guy can do tremendous damage, especially to a child! Although the breed, overall, deserves its nickname of "Gentle Giant" there are some Great Danes that do not. This is why you must buy from a reputable breeder who is willing to guarantee the temperament on the puppy.

DISQUALIFICATIONS

Danes under minimum height.

Split nose.

Docked tail.

Any color other than those described under "Color, Markings and Patterns."

None of the disqualifications (with perhaps the exception of poor temperament) disqualify any Great Dane from becoming a beloved member of the family!

About Temperament

As pointed out earlier, the Great Dane was once a fierce and aggressive dog. Early breeders worked miracles in improving the temperament by carefully selecting only those animals with milder, more tractable temperaments from which to breed. However, it's very important to remember that the genes for aggressiveness are still lurking in this dog's genetic background and if breeders aren't very careful about continuing to select for good temperament, they may create Danes that are less than ideal in this area.

Choose a Great Dane puppy with a consistently friendly and dependable temperament.

Although temperament is certainly influenced by environment, remember that basic temperament is considered by many to be inherited! Before you buy your puppy, ask the breeder about the dog's temperament. Ask what he or she considers to be the ideal temperament for the breed and ask to meet the dam and the sire if possible.

Inherited temperament traits can be greatly influenced by the way a dog is handled and by his environment. Young puppies need to be exposed to all kinds of stimuli. The breeder should be handling the puppies from birth, every day. They should not be isolated from everyday home life. Very young puppies should hear pots and pans clanging around, the TV playing and should see the faces of the family. Once the puppies are about 3 weeks old, they should have interaction with visitors. As long as guests have not been around other animals, and have washed their hands thoroughly, they may handle the puppies as well.

When the puppies are about 4 weeks old, they can wander in and out of their room and into an outdoor kennel run. They can also have supervised access to the home and have time to meet other dogs in the family. From the time they have sight, the puppies should be given lots of different toys. They can also be taken out of the home once they've had at least two parvovirus vaccines and one DHLP vaccine. When my puppies are a little older than 4 weeks, I take them to my friend's home to explore her outdoor playground of agility equipment.

Your Great Dane will be much more than a handsome dog—he'll be a loving and loyal friend.

No matter how good your new puppy's temperament is, it is up to you to properly socialize him. Once he's had his vaccines, take him to safe places where there are people who will pet him and give him lots of loving attention. You might wish to take along a treat to give strangers to offer him if he shows any signs of being a little wary of new people or situations. Another good way to socialize your pup is to enter him in puppy kindergarten classes and, when he's old enough, obedience classes. These issues will be discussed in greater detail in chapter 4.

With proper socialization, your big dog will be affectionate and gentle. The Great Dane is much more than his physical appearance. He's a heavy head in your lap looking into your face with adoring eyes. He's a large rear end planted firmly in your lap! He's a big, warm body who loves to be hugged and squeezed. He's a calm, abiding presence in your family. He'll be among the best and most loyal friends you'll ever have!

chapter 2

The Great Dane's Ancestry

Evidence of ancient dogs that were similar to the Great Danes we recognize today has been found among the excavations of ancient Assyrian artifacts. According to Di Johnson in *Great Danes Today,* "Two pictures of old Assyrian monuments are preserved to this day: One, a relief plate came from a Babylonian temple built 2,000 years B.C., showing an Assyrian man with a powerful Dane-like dog on a leash, while the second picture shows dogs pursuing two horses who have been hit by arrows. These dogs appear powerful specimens of boarhound type, not dissimilar to Great Danes as we know them." The early Assyrian culture was advanced and active in trade with other countries. It is believed that the Assyrians included some of their dogs with exported goods because the likeness of their dogs has been found in the artifacts of the ancient Romans and

Greeks. There is a Grecian coin in the Royal Museum at Munich that dates from the fifth century B.C. It depicts a likeness of a dog that greatly resembles the modern Great Dane.

Great Danes used to be well known as powerful hunting dogs.

A Hunting Hound

The early Great Dane, imported directly from Germany, was a large and powerful hunting hound. She was used as an effective war dog, guard and hunter of wild boar. The forests of Germany abounded with hundreds of wild boar, and large hunts were a common occurrence. The dogs' ears were cropped extremely short to prevent them from being injured when the dogs ran through heavy brush or encountered the razor sharp tusks of boars. The Great Danes of the past were aggressive and had a temperament that was very different from the "Gentle Giant" we know today.

It's interesting to note that the size of the early Great Dane was nowhere near today's average. According to *The Complete Great Dane* by Milo G. Denlinger, there was a dog named Harras v. Nero who stood 31.6 inches and a bitch, Juno, who stood only 29.6 inches. Today, these dogs would be considered almost too small to be competitive in conformation competition where bitches average 32 inches and dogs average 34 to 35 inches!

FAMOUS OWNERS OF THE GREAT DANE

Clara Bow

Sid Caesar

Mike Douglas

Edith Dutkin

Ruta Lee

Greg Louganis

Meredith Macrae

Olivia Newton-John

Valerie Perrine

Heritage

The modern Great Dane hails from Germany and England. No one seems to know how this huge dog came to be called the Great Dane as there's no evidence that she was ever popular in Denmark. In Germany, she was known as the Deutsche Dogge (German Dog).

Early German Danes were huge and had a coarse coat—more like that of the Mastiff than the present-day Great Dane. The Mastiff, Greyhound and Irish Wolfhound have all been credited as recent ancestors of the Great Dane. The evidence for Greyhound ancestry is apparent in the merle (black) coloration associated with the harlequin pattern seen in the breed today. According to Earnest Hart in *This Is The Great Dane,* ". . . for the patchy dark-on-a-white-ground coloring of the harlequin variety is a pattern derived from the Greyhound breeds throughout the Egyptian Greyhound, a direct descendent of the prototype dog, *Canis Familiaris Leineri.*"

Some believe that the title "tiger dog" derived from the brindled coat of some Great Danes.

FROM HUNTER TO HUGGER

The extremely aggressive temperament of the early Great Dane was almost unmanageable. Her use as a hunting dog by day, and guard dog by night, required this type of disposition. She continued to be so aggressive that the breed was banned from dog shows in the United States for several years. It is a great tribute to the early American breeders who recognized the importance of improving the Great Dane's demeanor. This was achieved within about twenty years of the first importation of Great Danes. Breeders were able to keep the desired guarding behavior that is still exhibited today by the Great Dane. Today she is basically the most gentle of dogs. Your Great Dane should be devoted to your family, and willing to accept anyone into your home who is welcomed by you.

The Great Dane's Color

The early Great Dane was sometimes referred to as the "tiger dog." This title prompted controversy because some authorities claimed that the name was derived from the striped effect of brindling, and others (particularly German breed historians) thought the Harlequin factor was the reason for the "tiger" title.

Because there was no "color code" in breeding Great Danes in those days, there was a veritable rainbow of colors to be found in the dogs. Fawn, blue, brindle, classical black and the white harlequin pattern abounded.

A Sensitive Breed

We can see from the comments of Mr. E. Mebter of Berlin, quoted from *The Complete Great Dane* by Denlinger, that there were many problems encountered in the early breeding of Great Danes. "I have bred Great Danes since 1875, and I do not believe it to be an over-statement to say that the Great Dane became popular in North Germany because of my kennel. As most people know, this breed is very sensitive because of the fine hair of its coat, and the breeding is very difficult. There are always heavy losses because of distemper, abortion, etc. In the year 1881 in two weeks time I lost forty young Great Danes through distemper, and in 1882 after the dog show at Hanover I lost fourteen grown Danes because of inflammation of the lungs. In the course of time I lost hundreds of puppies until I learned that the Great Dane is a 'hothouse plant' who must be carefully protected during his first year of life from catching cold. The chief cause of

Champion Dinro Taboo Again (L) with his son Champion Dinro Talisman (R).

21

distemper is a cold, and all my attempts to 'harden' my dogs against colds resulted in heavy losses."

Arrival in America

In 1857, Mr. Francis Butler imported the first Great Dane into the United States. This was a harlequin Dane from London named Prince. The first time Great Danes were shown in this country was in 1877 at the Philadelphia Grand National Show. They were then shown under the name of Siberian Bloodhounds, or Ulm dogs.

Ch. Calhoun of Tamerlane.

The Great Dane Club of America was formed in 1889. This club felt that this regal dog should be called the Great Dane, not Boarhounds, Ulm Dogs or Siberian Bloodhounds. Juno, a brindle bitch that was owned by the Osceola Kennel in Wisconsin, was the first Great Dane Champion listed in the Great Dane Club of America's records. Though the Westminster Kennel Club named a Great Dane as Best of Breed in 1887, it wasn't until 1889 that the AKC accepted and created the first American Standard for the breed. Over the years that followed, breeders largely invested in importing excellent lines of Great Danes (primarily from German kennels). Due to the dedication and commitment of Great Dane breeders, these magnificent dogs flourished. According to the American Kennel Club's Dog Registration Statistics, Great Danes ranked 29th, with 11,878 Great Danes and 3,526 Great Dane litters registered in 1997.

chapter 3

The **World**
According to the
Great Dane

Living with a Great Dane is, to say the least, a unique experience. Although your Great Dane may weigh as much or more than you weigh, and might tower over your head if he's standing on his hind legs, he has no idea that he is that big. He thinks he's a lap dog!

A Friendly Giant

People who visit my home and aren't familiar with Great Danes are always astounded by my dogs' temperament. Usually all of the dogs will be napping on their respective sofas or beds and will begrudgingly get up to come say "hi" to the visitor.

On occasion the visitors may be greeted by the four dogs barking at them.

24

Poppy, my 6-year-old Great Dane, *always* has to have something in her mouth. She'll run and find a stuffed toy and present it to the newcomer with a wagging tail, all the while "talking" to them by making a sound like a cartoon wolf: "Woo, woo, wooo, wooOOOOooo!"

AFFECTIONATE

Poppy's 10-year-old mother, Narcissus, will quietly limp up to visitors (she has arthritis) and lean affectionately against the nearest warm body, hoping to be petted. Narci's sister, Jonquilla, also must find a treasure to present to her new friend and will patiently stand in the background until someone notices her.

ENERGETIC

Skylark, Poppy's 3-year-old daughter, is the second youngest of the family. Lark is a very busy, high-energy dog! She likes to be right in your face. Although almost tall enough to look a person in the eye, this isn't good enough for Lark and she must spring up and down until she can get a good look at your face! Once she's got your attention, she, too, runs off to find a toy to offer. Last, but not least, is Skylark's baby daughter Gala. She usually runs around getting under foot and sometimes tripping an unsuspecting visitor.

Like many Great Danes, Poppy and Jonquilla love to recline on the family couch.

Have a Seat!

When visitors are ushered into the living room and seated comfortably on the sofas, they may soon find themselves with a Great Dane's behind in their lap. It's quite common for a Dane to back up into a lap or onto a sofa and plop his rear down while the forelegs continue to rest on the floor. Poppy does a variation of this. She'll stand next to the seated person, and then simply allow her body to fall sideways, pinning them under her body as she stretches out on top of them! If the dogs aren't sitting on you, they're probably begging for attention in some other manner, like sticking their noses in your face!

A Powerful Tail

Often the most dangerous end of a Great Dane is his tail. When he wags his tail, it can have a whiplike effect. A gentleman would do well to protect himself when around a Great Dane, and a child can be just the right height to get a good slap across the face. A Great Dane's tail has been known to efficiently clear a coffee table of its contents in one swipe.

The author and four generations of Great Danes: Skylark, Gala, Narcissus and Poppy.

Great House Dogs

Great Danes are generally quiet and clean house dogs. My Danes spend most of the day sleeping! But if they hear the car keys, or the word "cookie" or "walkie," they're right behind me! They are not a breed that you put in the backyard and never allow inside. One of my first requirements for potential puppy buyers is that they agree to primarily keep the dog in the house. Great Danes are especially easy to keep inside because they are quickly and easily housetrained, especially if you use a crate or a doggie door.

Because Great Danes have short hair, they are definitely *not* a breed you can keep outdoors year-round. They are house dogs and thrive when they are allowed to become part of the family. A Dane relegated to the backyard will be an unhappy dog. This isn't to say that they cannot stay outdoors while you're at work or absent. However, you must provide them with a shelter that will provide shade and protection from the hot sun in the summer, and warmth and protection from the elements in the winter. If you have a room in your home that can have a doggie door leading outdoors into a dog run, this would be ideal. If not, you must provide something similar for the dog's well-being.

About Destructive Chewing and Digging

Although a puppy is more inclined to destructive chewing than an adult, a Dane *can be* extremely destructive at any age.

As puppies, though they can be pretty rowdy, they can be trained to know where it's appropriate to play and where they need to be calm. It's a good idea to have a place where your Dane can be when you can't supervise him (such as a crate or an outdoor area with a shelter). A chewing Chihuahua isn't going to do anywhere near the same amount of damage that a Great Dane can do. When a Great Dane decides to chew up your sofa, it's usually gone.

Lots of training and close supervision may be necessary if your Great Dane tends to be destructive.

If you're a fastidious gardener, and want a picture-perfect backyard, you may want to consider whether a Great Dane is the right breed for you. If a Dane decides to dig, he will dig *very big* holes! When a Dane likes to play with the vegetation in the backyard, you might find a tree planted in your living room or the middle of your bed (as I did

27

once)! Even when they have a *huge* play area, they can find just the tree that they shouldn't. This doesn't necessarily mean that all Danes are destructive. It's just that if they *do* decide to do some damage, it's usually of major proportions! If you find that your dog has a tendency to dig or destructively chew, he will need lots of training and supervision.

Shedding

Like most breeds, Great Danes shed, but because they have a shorthaired coat, you won't see the volume of hair that you will with a longer haired breed. They "change" their coat in the spring, when the days begin to get longer. They shed again in the fall when the days become shorter. Because of their short coat, grooming is a breeze. My Danes get bathed either just before a show, or as needed, maybe every month or so.

Great Danes, which are short-haired, shed in the spring and fall.

Drooling

Drooling isn't a major problem with most Great Danes unless they're anticipating a treat or a meal. However, there *are* some lines of Great Danes or individual dogs that are considered to be "wet mouthed" (having a tendency to drool). If this is unpleasant for you, you should ask about this trait in both parents of the Great Dane you are considering bringing home. Many Danes will fling their saliva on your walls with ease, simply by shaking their heads. This attribute is due to their lips, which are much looser than many of the other breeds. If you find drooling offensive and bothersome, a Great Dane is probably not the right breed for you.

Along with drooling, Great Danes are also adept at carrying water in their mouths. My Danes seem to find it amusing to take a drink, hold most of the water in their mouths (their lips help) and innocently lay their heads on my lap. I usually end up with a very wet lap. Occasionally I'll get *mud* in my lap if my dogs also happened to have laid their faces in dirt.

Exercise

Because of the Great Dane's large size, many people think that this breed requires a lot of exercise. This is not necessarily true. Danes need two to three short walks every day, just like other breeds. A Great Dane can even do well in an apartment if his owner walks him several times daily and takes him to a fenced "dog park" where dogs can be safely allowed off lead to romp and play. Puppies, of course, will be able to get adequate exercise in the average backyard. If you wish to jog with your Dane, wait until he's at least 18 months old and then build him up to the distance gradually, just as you would for yourself.

Make sure that you don't encourage your dog to exercise vigorously when it's hot outside. Hot days are generally difficult for Great Danes; those with a dark-colored coat (black, blue and brindle) are more likely than light-colored dogs to suffer from heatstroke. It is extremely important to provide adequate shade and plenty of cool water if your dog must stay outdoors during hot weather.

> **GOT GAS?**
>
> Great Danes are not more gaseous than other breeds, but they're prone to gastric torsion (bloat). It's best to feed your dog a minimum of two meals daily. I feed my Danes a top-quality food that has a probiotic added (a combination of digestive enzymes and healthful digestive bacteria that aids in digestion). Since I've fed my dogs this way, there has been a marked decrease in my dogs' problems with gas.

Playing with a Puppy

Although Dane puppies are often larger than adult dogs of smaller breeds, they are actually quite fragile.

Because of their size and weight, a fall for a Great Dane puppy has the potential for greater damage than a fall for a smaller puppy of a different breed. Danes tend to break bones easily. Tug-of-war is a game that's fun for both the puppy and the owner but this game is ill-advised. Many believe that it teaches possessiveness and aggression in puppies; moreover, a rough jerk on the neck could have dire consequences for the puppy if his neck vertebrae are injured. Find less "competitive" games to play with your pup.

Great Dane puppies should be played with gently; their bones are fragile and are easily broken.

Don't do any kind of forced exercise with a puppy until he's at least 18 months old. Allow him all of the off-lead free play he wants (in an enclosed or safe area). Also allow him all of the downtime he wants. A puppy will sleep most of the day with brief periods of wakefulness and play time. A good deal of rest is important and necessary for a growing puppy. Many adult dogs also sleep or rest about twenty hours a day.

How Long Do Great Danes Live?

Great Danes live an average of about six to seven years, a shorter life span compared to other breeds. This is true of most giant breeds but doesn't mean that some Great Danes can't live longer (many do). My Great Danes tend to live about nine to ten years, and I've even had one live for twelve years. Why do I have Great Danes if they don't live very long? Because while I *do* have them, the joy of having them around is worth every tear shed when I lose one.

Health Problems of the Great Dane

Great Danes tend to have a lot of health problems (see chapter 7). You need to be aware of the potential for problems before you make the decision to own a Great Dane. The onset or severity of some health concerns can be mitigated by the way you raise the puppy and by the way you feed him during his fast-growth periods. Other health problems are simply inherited and there's not much to be done about them.

More Information on Great Danes

National Breed Clubs

Great Dane Club of America (GDCA)
Ms. Sue Mahany, Corresponding Secretary
11407 North Route 91
Dunlap, IL 61525
Phone: (309) 243-7054
Fax: (309) 698-3149
www.gdca.org

This is the AKC parent club for the Great Dane. They can give you information on all aspects of the breed, including the names and addresses of clubs in your area. Inquire about membership.

Books

Ackerman, Lowell. *Dr. Ackerman's Book of the Great Dane.* Neptune, New Jersey: TFH Publications, 1996.

Dye, Dan. *Amazing Gracie.* New York: Workman Publishing Company, 2000.

Johnson, Di. *Great Danes Today.* North Pomfret, Vermont: Trafalgar Square, 2000.

McCracken, Mary J. *The Great Dane Handbook.* Centreville, Alabama: OTR Publications, 1995.

Stahlkuppe, Joe. *Great Danes.* Hauppuage, New York: Barrons Educational Series, 1994.

Stern, G.B. *The Ugly Dachshund.* Exeter, New Hampshire: JN Townsend Publishers, 1998.

Swedlow, Jill. *Great Dane: Model of Nobility.* New York: Howell Book House, 1999.

MAGAZINES

The Great Dane Reporter
P.O. Box 150
Riverside, CA 92502-0150
Phone: (909) 784-5437}
FAX: (909) 369-7056
E-mail: gdr@pe.net
Web: www.gdr.com

Dane World Magazine
(Quarterly publication)
13318 Elk Run Road
Bealeton, VA 22712
Phone: (540) 439-2907
Web: www.daneworld.com

WEBSITES

Great Dane Home Page
www.ualberta.ca/~dc8/dane.htm

Visit this Web site for information on health issues particular to Danes, as well as fun features such as poetry and art.

The Great Dane Web Ring
www.daneweb.com/grtdane/greatring.html

For access to everything Great Dane, you must stop by this Web site. Sign up to join and soon you'll be privy to all sorts of Dane-related Web pages—from first-hand accounts of life as a Great Dane, to important health information.

Great Dane Rescue Alliance
www.gdrescuealliance.org

This extremely right-minded site supplies its own code of ethics for rescuing dogs, provides information for those wishing to start their own humane organization, and offers easy-to-follow guidelines for providing reputable doggie foster care.

Great Dane FAQ 1
www.ces.clemson.edu/~jshea/faq1.html

Stop by this Web site for a run down of general information on Danes including their personality traits, grooming needs, exercise and training particulars, ear cropping and health concerns.

Great Dane Links Directory
www.ginnie.com/gdlinks.htm

This is the everything Web site to guide you on a Dane-lover's tour of the Internet. With over 800 links in 10 categories, there's sure to be something for everyone.

Danes-R-Us
www.danesrus.com

This Web site is the place to go for fun Great Dane memorabilia such as note cards and post cards, a printable calandar and free Dane graphics.

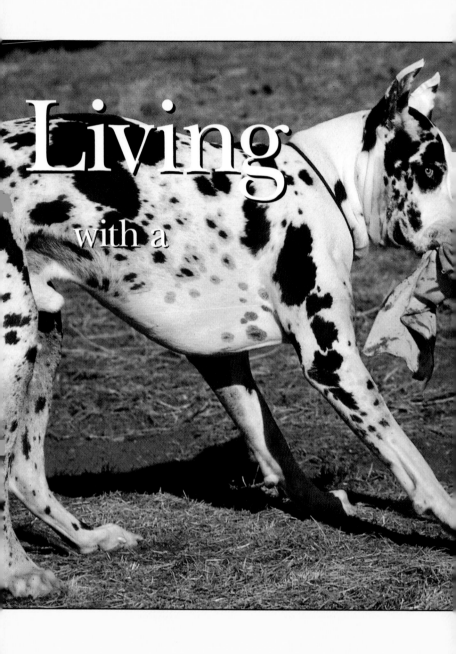

Living

with a

part two

Great Dane

chapter 4

Bringing Your
Great Dane
Home

The big day is here! Your new puppy is coming home. Are you ready? There are many special preparations you must do before your Great Dane's arrival. Remember that a very large puppy, that is going to get a whole *lot LARGER*, is joining your family!

Puppy-Proofing

Puppy-proofing a home for a Great Dane entails a lot of diligence. Great Dane puppies can reach a lot higher, wag a lot harder and take much bigger bites out of household items than most other pups. Think of this task as you would child-proofing. Take some time and go look through the house and rooms where the puppy will be allowed. Pay special attention to anything that could be harmful to your dog. Here is a list of safety measures that you should take to prevent your pup from being injured:

- Protect your puppy from electric cords and electric outlets. Child-proofing plugs should safeguard your Great Dane from possible electrocution. Electrical cords should be unplugged and kept high enough to be out of the puppy's reach.

- Tape or tie cord pulls for blinds and other window covers up high and out of the reach of your Great Dane. A curious puppy can easily get tangled in or practically hung by these cords.

- Teach your Great Dane at a young age not to paw at or jump against glass. Windows and sliding doors can be extremely dangerous to your Great Dane.

Great Danes should be taught when they are young not to lean on, paw at or jump against windows and sliding glass doors.

- When in the home or a securely fenced yard, do not leave a collar of any kind on your puppy or adult dog! Unless you get the kind of collar that will break away under stress, your dog can be seriously injured if the collar gets caught on something and doesn't give.

- Poisonous houseplants should not be kept in the household. If you want to keep your plants healthy you might want to keep them out of your dog's reach!

- Insecticides, herbicides, mouse bait, ant bait and any other poisonous substance should not be used in any area that your puppy or adult Dane might be. Poisonous substances sprayed on lawns can be picked up on feet, licked and ingested. Do not use any kind of floor cleaner that contains pine tar. This is also a toxic substance for dogs.

- Safeguard your cupboards or doors. Some Great Danes are very adept at getting into trouble and require even more precaution. You may want to consider a bungie cord on the refrigerator and baby locks on the cupboards and trash cans.

- If you have a swimming pool or pond, you must either fence it off from the puppy, or teach the puppy to swim and use the exit steps. Never leave a puppy unattended near a body of water.

It is important to have an area of your backyard fenced off to provide a safe play area for your Great Dane.

- Remove breakable or cherished items that are within the puppy's reach. Puppies like to jump up on things with their front feet and check out high areas such as countertops. Once your Great Dane is grown, *nothing* is safe on kitchen counters! Anything edible should go in the refrigerator, in a cupboard or on top of the refrigerator.

- A fenced yard or exercise area is a *must* for your Great Dane. This is for the safety of your dog and your yard. Make sure that there are no poisonous plants in your yard that the puppy might chew. Walk the yard and check for protruding nails, glass, metal or any object on which the puppy could harm herself. Make sure that there are no loose fence boards or holes under the fence through which she could escape. If you have areas in the garden where she could ruin plants or eat the veggies, fence this off and save yourself and your puppy some grief.

Puppy's First Day Home

From the first hour your new puppy enters your home, she must be taught exactly what to expect. This will teach her limits and what behaviors are acceptable. She'll be a happy dog if she knows what to do to earn praise from her beloved person.

If you can, bring home a small piece of urine-soiled newspaper from the breeders, and place it in the area of the yard where you want the puppy to relieve herself. This should be the very first activity upon arriving home. Stay with the puppy while she investigates, keeping her in this area until she relieves herself. Offer her lots of praise when she does.

Crate-Training

One of the best things you can do for you, your puppy or adult dog and your house is to crate-train your puppy while she's young. Dogs descend from animals that spent much time in the safe space of their dens. This is why it won't take long for your puppy to feel at home and safe in her dog crate. Returning home to a safely crated puppy is much better than returning home to damaged furniture and a messy carpet.

Every time you put your puppy into her crate, put a favorite treat or toy in the crate first. Very gently help your puppy into the crate and shut the door. Until she gets accustomed to the crate she may whimper, but if you walk away and don't take her out until she's settled down, she'll soon get used to it.

My dogs love their crate and use it as their very own "safe place" where they can get away from the bustle of the house and the kids. Once my puppies are old enough to spend time outdoors, I always keep a crate in the backyard for shelter. After playing for a while, they usually pile right in. It's like a little cave or den and seems to feel just right to them.

PUPPY ESSENTIALS

Your new puppy will need:

food bowl

water bowl

collar

leash

I.D. tag

bed

crate

toys

grooming supplies

A Dane (or any dog) should not be crated for most of the day and night. If the dog must stay alone all day, it is best to provide some way for the dog to move around and relieve herself. It is wise to have a familiar person check in on your Dane so she doesn't get too lonely.

You should already have a crate before you bring your puppy home. I recommend that you get a wire crate that is sized for an adult Dane. In the beginning, you can partition it off so it's only big enough for the puppy to comfortably lie down, stand and turn around. If the crate is too large, the puppy may be tempted to use a part of it as a relief area. With a smaller crate, she will cry when she needs to go out and you can quickly take her outside. A comfortable size for most Danes is about 48 inches long, by 36 inches high by 28 inches wide.

A puppy, of course, will need lots of guidance. She should not be in her crate for more than an hour without having an opportunity to eliminate. When she's out of the crate for short play periods, you should look out for signals that she needs to go out (crying and sniffing about). When she eliminates in the appropriate place, give her lots of praise. If you need to leave for work, put the pup where she will be spending the day—remember not to leave her in a crate for more than an hour at a time.

Supplies to Get Before Puppy Comes Home

In addition to a crate, there are important items to have in the home before your new puppy arrives.

FOOD AND DOG DISHES

Find out what your puppy is being fed at the breeders before you bring her home so you can have some food on hand when she arrives. Choose dog dishes that are easy to clean and are shaped or weighted so that they are difficult to tip over. Wash the food dish after each use (and the water dish once a day), and refill the water dish frequently. Because Great Danes grow to be so tall, it is best to purchase a food and water dish stand.

Toys

Toys are essential to the health of your Great Dane. Some of the best toys for a puppy are old gym socks knotted together. Dogs usually love plush stuffed toys from pet stores as well. If you give your Great Dane a ball, please make sure that it is size appropriate—not so small that it can get stuck in her throat. Tennis balls are fine for baby puppies, but too small for an adult Dane.

Something to Chew

All Danes need something to chew. This is essential when your Great Dane is teething and to help remove plaque and promote healthy gums. The very best chew items for a Dane are big, knobby bones that are made of hard nylon. Rawhide chews are not recommended because a chunk can be ripped off and caught in a dog's throat.

A soccer ball is the perfect size for a Dane.

Soft Beds

Because Great Danes are such large dogs, it's important to provide them with very soft, comfortable beds to protect their sharp elbows and the bony protrusions on their legs. Some of the fake fur beds lined with foam rubber work well. You can wash them easily, and they help to protect and prevent calluses. Please don't have your Great Dane lie on the bare floor, pieces of carpet (they chafe elbows and stifles) or cement. The softer the bed, the better.

Collars

When you first start your puppy on lead training, use a buckle-type collar and a 6-foot leather training lead. If your puppy is still in ear racks or has her ears taped, a buckle collar will be much easier to apply. Buy a collar that fits the puppy now and is adjustable for her quick and substantial growth. Once she's walking well on a buckle collar, you can switch to a soft nylon or chain choke collar. Just remember, this should *not* be left on at all times. If you're worried about identification if she should get lost, either have her tattooed or microchipped.

BABY GATES

Baby gates can be handy when you want your puppy with you but want to confine her to certain areas. Dog supply catalogs and retail stores carry baby gates at reasonable prices. Believe it or not, most Great Danes are not jumpers and will stand obediently behind a barrier that only comes up to their chest.

What to Ask the Breeder

Before you leave your breeder's home, discuss your puppy's health and any concerns you may have. The breeder should give you a list of the vaccines the puppy has had and when they were given. You should also discuss when the next vaccines are necessary. Ask for information about fecal checks and if the puppy was wormed. If she was wormed, take note of the parasite that was found and what treatment was used. There should be information including exactly how much (and what kind of) food she was being given and how often. Ask the breeder to fill you in on some of the possible problems a Great Dane puppy might encounter during fast-growth periods. If you have medical

---

HOUSEHOLD DANGERS

Curious puppies and inquisitive dogs get into trouble not because they are bad, but simply because they want to investigate the world around them. It's our job to protect our dogs from harmful substances, like the following:

IN THE HOUSE

cleaners, especially pine oil

perfumes, colognes, aftershaves

medications, vitamins

office and craft supplies

electric cords

chicken or turkey bones

chocolate

some house and garden plants, like ivy, oleander and poinsettia

IN THE GARAGE

antifreeze

garden supplies, like snail and slug bait, pesticides, fertilizers, mouse and rat poisons

---

questions about your puppy, it would be a good idea to consult both your veterinarian and the breeder.

Picking Out Your Puppy

When it is time to actually pick your puppy, try to avoid taking home the puppy that hangs back in the corner and refuses to come up to you. She might look sweet and cute, but she's not going to have a very outgoing temperament. It is likely that she's shy and will need a *lot* of work before she'll be comfortable in everyday situations. Without a lot of training and socialization, some shy dogs turn into fear biters. Also try to avoid the puppy that charges up to you and bites you on the chin. This is probably the alpha dog, or the "boss," of the litter. Unless you're well prepared to teach this dog that she is *not* the boss, and you don't have small children, this dog is probably not your wisest choice. You want to choose the puppy that comes willingly, with her tail high and wagging, right up to your chest to give you a kiss on the face, or to snuggle contentedly against you. This is the puppy who will be submissive enough to follow your lead, but confident enough to find life a fun adventure.

Great Danes and Children

Preparing for the new puppy should also include preparing the children. Different ages of children and Danes should be managed accordingly. Obviously you aren't going to leave the puppy and the kids unattended under *any* circumstances. This is simply asking for trouble. When we hear of instances of dogs biting children, very often it is due to mismanagement on the part of the children's parents.

Great Danes tend to view small children as littermates. If you've ever observed a litter of puppies, you will notice that much of their play behavior consists of the use of their teeth. This behavior helps puppies learn to inhibit the force of their bite. When they hurt a littermate, that puppy either yelps in pain or bites the other puppy back. The instigator has learned a valuable lesson. It takes a few times but eventually they learn the lesson. Adult dogs may still use their mouths during play, only more gently. Often dogs that have *not* learned this lesson are the dogs that become biters later in life.

As a parent and new puppy owner you have a responsibility to your children and to your Dane puppy. It is beneficial to teach both children and dogs what is and is not allowed. Kids should be taught not to hit or poke the puppy, not to throw things at her, and not to pull or push her around. They need to know that the puppy needs lots of quiet sleep in her private crate and that they are not to bother her during her naps. They should also be taught how to react when she bites them in play. Tell the child to yell "Ouch!" (just like a littermate would do) but not to hit the puppy or react in a violent way.

Children and dogs can become great friends, but they should always be supervised when together.

The puppy should also be taught her limits. Puppies need to be reminded not to bite! If your puppy bites you, try to react as mentioned above for children. A dog will understand the loud yelp of pain and a loud "No!" Try to avoid using a soft voice ("no, no, no . . .") and too many corrections. One very firm correction will impress her a lot more than a flurry of mild ones. The latter may create an unruly dog. When the puppy bites in play, provide her with a toy as a substitute for your hand or arm. By the time she's 5 or 6 months old, she should understand what is expected of her.

Socializing Your Great Dane

As soon as your puppy is safely vaccinated, it is important to routinely take her out into the world. Proper socialization includes getting the puppy used to street sounds and smells, new people, animals and objects. The people and animals that you choose to introduce her to should be friendly and gentle. Take your puppy for walks (on-lead) where she can see bicycles, shopping carts and runners; on car rides (not just to the groomer or veterinarian); and to places with varied footing such as grass, carpet, concrete and tile. If you are not sure where to start, check out the many dog clubs and obedience schools that have kindergarten puppy classes for socializing puppies.

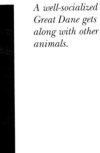

A well-socialized Great Dane gets along with other animals.

Start Training Early

Your Great Dane is most open to learning in the first few months of her life. With or without your input, I guarantee you that the puppy *will* learn something! *What* she learns depends on *you!* You should start training your Dane long before she's 5 or 6 months old. The more time you let pass before training your dog, the more challenging it will be to train her. (See chapter 8 for more on training.)

Protective Measures

It is *vital* that your dog always wear some sort of I.D. The rabies tag alone is useless, since it can't be traced should your dog get lost. Your pet's I.D. tag should contain your pet's name as well as your name and phone number. The Great Dane Club of America has a rescue representative in almost every part of this country. If you lose your Great Dane, call the American

Kennel Club and they can put you in touch with some-one in your area (or the area where your Great Dane was lost) who will be only too willing to help you and get the word out to be on the lookout for your pet.

The best I.D. is a tattoo placed on the inner thigh of a hind leg. Most dogs are tattooed with their owner's social security number. Many dog breed clubs run tat-too clinics. Check for one in your area. Your local vet-erinarian should be able to steer you in the right direction. It is a relatively painless procedure when done by a professional used to tattooing dogs.

There is also a microchip that can be painlessly in-serted into the dog's muscle, between the shoulder blades. The drawback to this is that you need a scanner to read the chip, and if your dog is found by a person who does not know how to do this, your pet might not be returned.

The single best preventative measure that one can take to ensure that a dog is not lost or stolen is to provide her with a completely fenced in yard. Check the fence periodically for digging spots or weakened structure.

chapter 5

Feeding
Your
Great Dane

Good nutrition is essential to the health of your Great Dane. It helps keep his coat healthy, reduces his susceptibility to disease, helps ward off infections and keeps him full of vigor.

Perhaps one of the most important aspects of raising a Great Dane is how and what you feed him. You must be aware that this dog grows as much in one year as many humans do in

eighteen years. When a dog's bones and tissues are forming this quickly, it's important that the dog receive the proper nutrients in the proper amounts, and that he receives the right combinations for each stage of growth. It is most important to provide your puppy with a top-quality food that is complete and balanced to support his body's rapid growth.

Nutrition Options

Some people feel that a home-cooked diet, one that follows recipes formulated by qualified nutritionists, is the ideal diet for a Great Dane. There are some good books on this under the category of natural feeding. Others believe in feeding high-quality dog foods that contain only *human grade* ingredients. A more specific dietary option is to feed your Great Dane a specially formulated diet, such as one that is 23 percent protein and 12 percent fat. This is usually fed to a dog if he is engaged in high-energy activities or is in a high-stress situation such as being bred or being shown. Additionally, if you are feeding your dog kibble, many owners find that adding a small amount of high-quality canned food helps improve the taste of the meal.

You'll know your Great Dane is eating right if his coat is shiny, his skin is supple and he's in high spirits, like these Great Danes.

It is important to give your Great Dane the highest quality diet that you can provide. When shopping for dog food, read the labels. Try to stay away from chemical preservatives (such as ethoxyquin, BHA and BHT). Dog labels list the ingredient that comprises the highest percentage of the food first. The first ingredients listed should be foods such as whole chicken, turkey or lamb. Try to avoid products that list by-products as protein. Skin problems and health problems can often be traced directly to inadequate nutrition. Consult with your veterinarian about your dog's diet if you notice skin problems or have questions about the food you're feeding him.

What's in Your Dog's Meal?

All dogs should be fed food that contains the appropriate amounts of digestible proteins, carbohydrates, fats, vitamins and minerals.

Protein is essential for bone growth, tissue healing, supporting amino acids and for the daily renewal of body tissues metabolized by regular activity. Protein is not stored in your dog's system, so he should be fed some source of protein every day.

Carbohydrates provide energy, help assure the proper absorption of fats and aid digestion and elimination. Excess carbohydrates are stored in the body as fat for future use.

Fats are a source of energy and also add shine to the dog's coat and suppleness to his skin. But excess fat is stored in the body tissues and may result in an overweight dog. Balancing fat intake is important—too much leads to problems associated with obesity, while too little contributes to skin and coat problems, insufficient insulation and decreased energy.

Vitamin A is used by the dog's body for fat absorption and is therefore necessary for a healthy, shiny coat. It also promotes a normal growth rate, healthy reproduction and good eyesight.

B vitamins act as a buffer to the nervous system and are essential for normal skin, eyes, growth, appetite and coat.

Vitamin D ensures healthy bones, teeth and muscle. It must be taken in the correct ratio with calcium and phosphorus to be effective.

Vitamin E helps with muscle function and with the operation of the internal and reproductive organs.

Vitamin K is essential for normal blood clotting to occur. If your dog has any problems with excessive bleeding, it should be reported to his veterinarian. This could point to a lack of vitamin K or a more acute problem.

Calcium and phosphorus must be present in the diet and in the correct ratio to protect puppies from rickets, bowed legs and other bone deformities. They also aid in muscle development and maintenance.

Your Great Dane's Diet

When you pick up your puppy from his breeder, ask questions about his current diet and feeding schedule. Your breeder will probably have some recommendations for you—feel free to ask for advice as well.

As a rule, most breeders don't supplement a nursing puppy's diet until he is about 4 weeks old. When the puppy is about 5 weeks old, he is gradually weaned onto a milk replacer and then introduced to solids. Soaked kibble is then provided with a small amount of canned meat. Once a Great Dane puppy's fast growth begins, most breeders reduce the dietary protein in his diet. This reduction of protein helps to prevent the puppy from growing too fast. When the dog is fully grown, at about 1½ years, it is not as important to worry about a higher protein diet.

HOW MUCH AND WHEN TO FEED

From puppyhood to adulthood, most Great Danes do best on *at least two meals a day*. Small, frequent feedings usually help to prevent bloat. It is also advisable to add a small amount of water to kibble and let it stand and expand before feeding it to the dog. Some breeders also recommend avoiding soy, as it tends to increase the occurrence of bloat.

As do most people, dogs thrive on a schedule. If 5 p.m. rolls around and I'm not making motions like I'm about to get dinner going, there are five wet noses that will prompt me! My Danes are on a feeding schedule (usually three meals a day). It is recommended that Great Danes should be fed more than twice daily due to problems with bloat. Once you establish a schedule, stick to it.

How much and when you feed your Great Dane is largely an individual decision. Consider where you live, how much exercise your Great Dane is getting and how much he tends to eat. He should receive at least two daily feedings of 2½ to 4 cups of kibble with either some canned food or table scraps, depending on sex, age, size and body condition. Depending on your dog's digestive system, provide fresh fruits and vegetables with discretion. Some dogs enjoy raw carrots as well as grapes, broccoli, apples, bananas and watermelon. However, since dogs have difficulty digesting the cellulose in fruits and vegetables, consider them a chew treat rather than food. If your dog has this problem, it is best to avoid adding such food to his diet.

Assessing Your Puppy

As your Great Dane puppy grows, his body should be kept lean regardless of the diet that you decide to feed him. It is more important to assess his body condition than to worry about what he weighs for his age. If you can *just* see his ribs and he's happy and active, he's most likely at an appropriate weight. It is important to keep your puppy at a healthful weight because an overweight puppy is more prone to developing maladies such as hip dysplasia, osteochondrosis dessicans, panosteoitis, wobblers syndrome and hypertrophic osteodystrophy. (These health concerns will be discussed in chapter 7.)

Where to Feed Your Great Dane

Feeding your puppy in the same place every day will help encourage a consistent routine. Because Great Dane puppies and adults are so tall and because they have problems with bloat, it is important to elevate their food dishes off of the floor (to the dogs' shoulder height). This can be done by putting the food bowls on a low box (while he's young) or on a folding chair. There are also special stands that hold two bowls, one for food and one for water. Elevating the bowls helps to minimize the amount of air that the dog takes in as he eats. Decreasing the amount of air that gets trapped in the dog's stomach decreases the possibility of bloating. Elevating the bowls also makes it more comfortable for older Danes who may have trouble bending down to the floor. Remember to have fresh, cool water available to your Great Dane at all times.

Elevating your Great Dane's food and water bowls helps decrease bloat and alleviates muscle strain.

Feeding Concerns

If your new puppy doesn't clean his bowl the first couple of times you feed him, don't be too concerned. Suddenly he's found himself in a new home, with new people, perhaps new critters, new smells and new sounds. Where have his littermates gone? Where's his mom? His breeder? Give your puppy lots of love and attention and you will see just how quickly he will adjust to his new environment.

Anytime a growing dog stops eating, it should be regarded as a cause for concern. While it is not unusual for a dog to skip a meal occasionally for no apparent reason, any extended period of food refusal calls for some medical attention. First, take the dog's temperature. Use a rectal thermometer and keep it inserted for however long the manufacturer advises. A dog's normal temperature is about 101.5°F. Any significant deviation is a cause for investigation. Check the dog's stool to rule out diarrhea, constipation or other digestive disorders. If you take your Dane to the veterinarian, be sure to bring a stool sample, which is very helpful in diagnosing illness.

Some people like to add flavorings to the food of a picky eater to stimulate the appetite. However, if you are dealing with an otherwise healthy pet, you may come to regret such a move. A dog or puppy that just stops eating without an underlying health reason, should be allowed to go hungry. No chicken broth, no treats, no nothing. When Bismarck gets hungry enough, he'll eat.

chapter 6

Grooming
Your
Great Dane

Grooming your Great Dane can be an enjoyable and relaxing part of your daily routine. Daily care will keep your Dane's coat in tip-top shape and, more importantly, will help her feel good. It's the perfect way to strengthen the bond between you and your dog. Do-it-yourself grooming will also save you money. Checking your Great Dane for bumps, external parasites, injuries and skin problems while grooming is an important preventative health step. Although Great Danes are really easy to groom, there are some important grooming tasks that must be maintained to ensure your dog's health and well-being.

Teaching Pup to Accept Grooming

It is best to begin grooming tasks, especially clipping nails and cleaning teeth, while your puppy is young. This will get her used to grooming and will be something for you both to look forward to. Your Great Dane will need to be taught that she must behave when she is being groomed. If your puppy gets unruly when handled any part of her body, tell her "No" in a firm voice. As she matures you will find that she'll become more cooperative and easier to handle.

Because Great Danes are so large, a grooming table may not be a practical option for you. You can groom your Great Dane as she stands patiently on the floor for you, or you can have her lie down on her side (on a *well-cushioned* surface). Remember to give her abundant praise for her obedience.

Grooming Toenails

Toenails are too long if they make clicking sounds on the floor when the dog walks or if they touch the ground when she is standing still. Dogs who have very long nails usually walk on the back of their feet, which leads to splayed toes and an unsteady gait. This is dangerous and uncomfortable for the dog. Left untrimmed, the toenails eventually curl under the foot and circle back (eventually piercing the pads). Clipping the nails once a week or every other week should maintain the proper nail length. You can trim the nails by using a nail clipper or a nail grinder.

When clipping your Great Dane's toenails, lift her foot up and forward; then hold it in your left hand so that your right hand is free to trim the nail. (You may, of course, trim with your left hand if you are left-handed.) Before you start trimming, locate the blood vessel called the quick in the bottom stem of the nail. If your Dane has light-colored nails, it should be fairly easy to see the quick just by looking through the nail. It may be a challenge to see the quick if your Dane has darker nails—to be safe, use a strong light and trim very small amounts at a time. Try to be very careful not to cut into the quick of the nail, as this will cause it to bleed. If you are uncomfortable trimming your Dane's nails the first time, have your veterinarian show you the quick and how he trims nails before you attempt to do it.

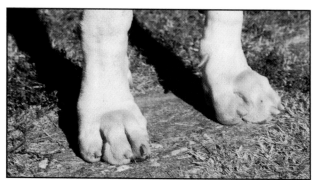

Another option for trimming nails is to use an electric or battery-powered nail grinder. Introduce your Great Dane to the noise that a nail grinder makes before you actually use it on her nails. A grinder is a safe way to trim nails with less chance for accidental bleeding. You can find grinders at many pet stores and through pet supply catalogs.

Cleaning Teeth

Regular teeth cleaning is important to the well-being of your Great Dane. To check your dog's teeth for tartar, hold her head firmly in one hand, and use the other hand to lift her lips upward. You can remove discoloration on the teeth by using a soft toothbrush or damp towel dipped in baking soda. Your veterinarian can do deeper teeth cleaning for stains you aren't able to remove yourself. Nylon bones and chew toys as well as hard dog biscuits will help remove plaque and keep your Great Dane's teeth white.

Coat Care

Because Great Danes have short hair, you don't have to worry about tangles and matting. A daily brushing along with good nutrition should keep your Dane's coat shiny. Most Danes will shed twice yearly. During this time, the hair will continue to fall for several weeks. You can help the shedding along by using a rubber curry comb or a rubber mitt. This pulls out all the loose hairs and your Great Dane will probably *love* being brushed!

Regular brushing will keep your Great Dane looking her best. It will also help you find any minor skin problems before they become severe.

Bath Time

Giving your Great Dane a bath is quite easy, and because brushing your dog's coat daily removes dirt and body odor, your Great Dane will rarely need a bath.

To prepare for a bath, gather some old clothes (to protect yourself from the inevitable shake-off), a tub (or a hose if it's warm weather), a spray-nozzle attachment for the hose, pH-balanced dog shampoo or a flea and tick dip if necessary, coat conditioner, cotton balls, washcloths, mineral oil and lots of large towels.

Before you bathe your Dane, give her a quick once-over with a towel or brush.

57

Before bath time, take your Dane out for some exercise and to eliminate. This will alleviate her desire to dash outside to do her business (and inadvertently take a roll in the dirt) just after you bathed her. Also, give her a good brushing just before you bathe her.

Take care to gently clean your Great Dane's ears during her bath.

The bath water should be warm, but not too hot. (Be sure to test the temperature before you begin.) Start by putting cotton balls in her ears to protect them from water. Then spray water all over her body except for her head and face. Put a dime-sized amount of shampoo on her back and massage her coat until you work up a good lather.

If you accidentally get soap in your Great Dane's eyes, apply a few drops of mineral oil in the inner corner of each eye to relieve discomfort. Rinse off the shampoo with the hose, then shampoo her again. Next, rinse very thoroughly, taking care to get all of the shampoo out of the dog's coat. Apply conditioner as the product recommends. If you are using a flea and tick dip or shampoo, consult with your veterinarian before applying it to your dog.

Once all of the shampoo is rinsed out, wipe your Dane's face and head with a damp washcloth. Take out the cotton balls from her ears and then wipe the ears with fresh cotton balls dipped in a small amount of mineral oil. Then wrap the large towels around your Great Dane and gently dry her off. Try to keep your Dane inside for a few hours to let her coat completely dry and to keep her clean.

All Around Good Looking

First and foremost it is important that your Great Dane be healthy and fit—grooming is like "the icing on the cake." A good-looking dog eats high-quality food, exercises regularly, and is clean and free of parasites. One of the first signs of an unhealthy dog may be a brittle coat that lacks shine. Regular grooming will help keep your Great Dane healthy and handsome.

Grooming your dog regularly is important to her overall health and well-being.

chapter 7

Keeping Your
Great Dane
Healthy

The best way for you to help your Great Dane lead a healthy life is to give him regular attention. Even the strongest body and the best genetic background can't replace an owner's loving care.

Dogs do not have a natural immunity to parasites, infections and many diseases. It is up to you to take preventative measures to ensure that your dog's health is not affected by these maladies. It is helpful to think of the upkeep of your dog's health in relation to the calendar. Record what needs to be done on a weekly, monthly and yearly basis.

A great way to keep informed of your Great Dane's health is through your dog's daily grooming sessions. The condition of his coat and skin and the "feel" of his body can tell you if he is in good health or has potential problems. When you are brushing or running your hands over your Great Dane, check for small lumps on or under the skin that have not become large enough to be seen without close examination.

Grooming is also the time to check for fleas and ticks. Depending on where you live and the season, these pests can be your dog's worst health problem. Besides being an extreme irritant to some dogs, fleas and ticks harbor diseases and parasites. If you can't see actual fleas, their existence can be confirmed by small black specks in the dog's coat. These specks are flea feces; when a dog is bathed, they dissolve and turn the bath water a rust color.

Flea Control

Flea control is a true challenge. The flea lives outside and hops on the dog not only for travel purposes but also for nutrition. Dogs bring fleas inside, where they lay eggs in the carpeting and furniture— anywhere your dog goes in the house. Therefore, the way to control fleas is by not only treating the dog but also the other environments

the flea inhabits. The yard can be sprayed, and in the house, sprays and flea bombs can be used. There are several options for your dog. Flea sprays are effective for one to two weeks depending on their ingredients. Dips applied to the dog's coat after a bath are also effective for about one to two weeks. The drawback to these methods is that some dogs don't respond well to the chemicals.

> ### FIGHTING FLEAS
>
> Remember, the fleas you see on your dog are only part of the problem—the smallest part! To rid your dog and home of fleas, you need to treat your dog *and* your home. Here's how:
>
> • Identify where your pet(s) sleep. These are "hot spots."
>
> • Clean your pets' bedding regularly by vacuuming and washing.
>
> • Spray "hot spots" with a nontoxic, long-lasting flea larvicide.
>
> • Treat outdoor "hot spots" with insecticide.
>
> • Kill eggs on pets with a product containing insect growth regulators (IGRs).
>
> • Kill fleas on pets per your veterinarian's recommendation.

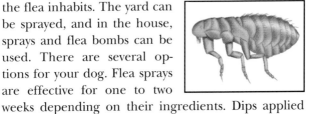

The flea is a die-hard pest.

Living with a
Great Dane

Flea collars help to prevent fleas from traveling to your dog's head, where it's moister and more hospitable. Check the length of effectiveness of you dog's flea collar and don't forget to apply a new collar when necessary. Again, some dogs have problems with flea collars, and children should never be allowed to handle them.

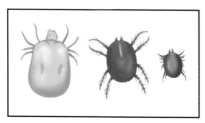

Three types of ticks (l-r): the wood tick, brown dog tick and deer tick.

Another option is a product that works from the inside out. Your veterinarian can apply a chemical to a spot on your dog's coat. The chemical is absorbed into the dog's body and works for up to a month to repel fleas. Another such option is a pill (prescribed by a veterinarian) that you give to the dog on a regular basis in his food. The chemicals in the pill course through the dog's bloodstream, and when the flea bites, the blood kills the flea.

Going over your Great Dane's coat every day with a flea comb (a fine-toothed comb) is also very helpful.

Use tweezers to remove ticks from your dog.

Deciding the course of action for controlling your dog's flea problem should be based on how much of a problem fleas are for the dog in question and what you feel most comfortable using.

Ticks

As you examine your Great Dane, also check for ticks that may have lodged in his skin, particularly around the ears or in the hair at the base of the ear, the armpits or around the genitals. If you find a tick, which is a small insect about the size of a pencil eraser when engorged with blood, smear it thoroughly with petroleum jelly. As the tick suffocates in the petroleum jelly, it will back out and you can then grab it with tweezers and kill it. If the tick doesn't back out, grab it with tweezers and slowly pull it out, twisting very gently. Don't just grab and pull or the tick's head may separate from the body. If the head remains in the skin, an infection or abscess may result and veterinary treatment may be required.

A word of caution: Don't use your fingers or fingernails to pull out ticks. Ticks can carry a number of diseases, including Lyme disease, Rocky Mountain spotted fever and others, all of which can be very serious.

Brushing Teeth

Another weekly job is brushing the teeth—this becomes more important as your dog ages. When a dog is young he's likely to spend a lot of time chewing: The teeth tend to stay clean this way.

Calcium deposits accumulate mainly on the back upper molars but spread to all teeth excluding the incisors in older dogs. These deposits are known

Check your dog's teeth frequently and brush them regularly.

as tartar (or calculus) and are the leading cause of gum disease, which leads to the eventual loss of teeth. Daily brushing helps to slow down this process, but even regular brushing doesn't completely stop the formation of tartar.

Having your dog's teeth cleaned twice a year at a veterinary clinic will help prolong the health of his mouth. You can also keep on top of early signs of oral cancer or infection by checking the mouth regularly for broken teeth and the formation of abnormalities.

Ear Care

Ears should also be cleaned on a weekly basis. Great Danes, especially those with cropped ears, do not have the ear problems common to dogs with long pendulous or hairy ears. However the moist environment created by uncropped ears that hang over the opening is an easy place for infections to incubate.

You can tell that your Great Dane has an ear problem if he scratches his ears or shakes his head frequently. Clean ears are less likely to develop problems, and if something does come up, it will be noticed while treatment can be done easily. If a dog's ears are very dirty and need to be cleaned on a daily basis, it is a good indication that something else is happening in the ears besides ordinary dirt and the normal accumulation of earwax. You should visit the veterinarian if this occurs—your dog may need special medication.

Checking Anal Sacs

A dog's anal sacs are located under the skin on both sides of the anal opening. The sacs fill with a thin, light brown fluid that is very malodorous. Removing the fluid in anal sacs is called *expressing*. These should be checked periodically; a good time to express the anal sacs is during the dog's bath.

You'll know that your dog is having trouble with his anal sacs when he scoots on his bottom across the floor. When the sacs are impacted they become swollen, and the fluid looks very dark and viscous. Serious impaction can lead to infection and may require surgery. Needless to say, this is not very comfortable for the dog.

The sacs are expressed by placing the thumb and the index and third fingers of one hand on both sides of the outer edge of the anus. Strong inward squeezing pressure on both sides of the anus at the same time usually removes the contents of the sac. A paper towel should be kept in the hand that is squeezing to collect the fluid.

Vaccines

Yearly vaccinations are essential to protect your dog from common deadly diseases. The DHL vaccine, which protects a dogs from distemper, hepatitis and leptospirosis, is given for the first time at about 7 weeks of age. Another booster is given a few weeks later. After this, your dog should be vaccinated every year throughout his life.

Parvovirus and coronavirus have been the cause of death for thousands of dogs since the 1970s. These illnesses most frequently affect puppies and older dogs. Fortunately, vaccines for parvovirus and coronavirus are given on a yearly basis in combination with the DHL shot.

KENNEL COUGH

Kennel cough is a condition of the respiratory system that can be caused by any number of different viral or bacterial agents. Though rarely dangerous, it is highly contagious and is easily spread in a kennel situation where there are many dogs confined to a restricted space. The most obvious symptom is a cough caused by inflammation of the trachea, bronchi and/ or lungs. Antibiotics may be prescribed to prevent pneumonia and a cough suppressant may quiet the cough. Most cases are mild and many dogs recover spontaneously having received no treatment whatsoever. The Bordatella vaccine, given twice a year, will protect a dog from getting most strains of kennel cough. It is not routinely given, so it may be necessary to request it for your Great Dane.

> **YOUR PUPPY'S VACCINES**
>
> Vaccines are given to prevent your dog from getting an infectious disease like canine distemper or rabies. Vaccines are the ultimate preventive medicine: They're given before your dog ever gets the disease so as to protect him from the disease. That's why it is necessary for your dog to be vaccinated routinely. Puppy vaccines start at 8 weeks of age for the five-in-one DHLPP vaccine and are given every three to four weeks until the puppy is 16 months old. Your veterinarian will put your puppy on a proper schedule and will remind you when to bring in your dog for shots.

LYME DISEASE

Lyme disease is a bacterial disease caused by a spirochete (*Borrelia Burgdorfen*) and is spread through direct contact with the tiny deer tick. Most tick bites result in an area of red swelling, but the Lyme-infected bite is particularly large, long-lasting and painful. Later symptoms include lameness, fatigue and eventual death. There is a protective available for dogs—ask your veterinarian if this is something your dog needs. Always check yourself and your dog for ticks after an outing in grass or woods.

Internal Parasites

The inside of the dog's body is commonly inhabited by a variety of parasites. Most of these are in the worm family and include tapeworms, roundworms, whipworms, hookworms and heartworm. There are also several types of protozoa, mainly *coccidia* and *giardia,* that cause problems for dogs.

The common **tapeworm** is acquired by the dog that eats infected fleas or lice. In the adult stage, the worm inhabits the intestine, where it sucks the nutrients it needs from the dog. The only clues that your dog has tapeworms are if he has a dull coat, a loss of weight despite a good appetite or infrequent gastrointestinal problems.

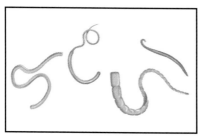

Common internal parasites (l-r): roundworm, whipworm, tapeworm and hookworm.

Confirmation of tapeworm is by the presence of worm segments in the stool. These appear as small, pinkish-white, flattened rectangular-shaped pieces. They look like rice when dry. If segments are not present, diagnosis can be made by a discovery of eggs when a stool sample is examined under a microscope. The veterinarian can prescribe worming medicine to temporarily rid the dog of tapeworm. Over-the-counter medication is not recommended and may be dangerous to your dog. The presence of the host fleas or lice must be handled before long-term tapeworm can be controlled.

Ascarids are the most common **roundworm** (nematode) found in dogs. There are rarely symptoms exhibited in adult dogs that would indicate that they have roundworm. These cylindrical worms may be as long as 4 to 5 inches. They pose the greatest danger to puppies, where they are usually passed from the mother through the uterus to the unborn puppies.

Heavy infestations will appear in puppy stools, though a stool sample is the best way to diagnose roundworm. Treatment is easy and can be started as early as 2 weeks of age and given every two weeks thereafter until eggs no longer appear in a stool sample or dead worms are not found in the stool following treatment.

Hookworms are generally found in warmer climates, and infestation is generally from ingestion of larvae from the ground or penetration of the skin by larvae. Hookworms feed in the dog's intestine and can cause anemia, diarrhea and emaciation. These worms are not visible to the eye—their diagnosis must be made by a veterinarian.

Whipworms live in the large intestine and cause few if any symptoms. Infestation is from ingestion of larvae from contaminated soil. Diagnosis and treatment should be made by a veterinarian. All dog owners can help control these parasites by picking up dog stool on a daily basis. This will help keep the soil from being infested.

The protozoa are more challenging to diagnose and treat. *Coccidia* and *giardia* are the most common, and mainly affect young puppies. Unsanitary, overcrowded conditions, the premises themselves (soil), water or an infected mother (if she is a carrier) are usually associated with these protozoa.

A healthy Great Dane is full of energy.

The most common symptom of a protozoan infection is mucous-like, blood-tinged feces. Diagnosis of this condition can only be made with freshly collected samples of feces. With coccidia, besides diarrhea, the puppies will appear to be listless and with little appetite. Puppies often harbor the protozoa and show no symptoms unless they are experiencing stress. Consequently, puppies will often not present symptoms until they go to a new home. Once diagnosed, treatment is quick and effective and the puppy returns to good health almost immediately.

Heartworm

Heartworm is the most serious of the common internal parasites. A dog that is bitten by a mosquito infected with the heartworm *microfilaria* (larvae) will develop worms that are 6 to 12 inches long. As these worms mature they take up residence in the dog's heart.

The symptoms of heartworm often include coughing, tiring easily, difficulty breathing and weight loss. Heart failure and liver disease may eventually occur. Blood testing and screening for the microfilaria is necessary to confirm a heartworm infection.

Regardless of how cute puppies may be, it is rarely a good idea to allow your dog to breed. Have your Great Dane spayed or neutered.

If you live in an area where heartworm is prevalent, it is best to place your dog on a preventative treatment. Because the microfilaria and mosquitoes require warm temperatures to propagate, concern for heartworm transmission is limited to the warmer months of the year. Consequently, many owners only give their dogs the heartworm preventative for a portion of the year. Anytime a dog is taken off heartworm treatment and then placed back on it, he must have his blood checked to make sure he is not harboring heartworm.

It is crucial that your dog is given a full veterinary treatment at least once a year. His overall condition can be checked and a blood sample taken for a complete screening. This way the dog's thyroid functions can be tested, and the dog's organs can be monitored. This is the best way to prevent disease and take care of small problems while they are easy to treat.

Excellent care, regular examinations, periodic stool checks and preventive medications for conditions such as heartworm will all promote your dog's good health.

Spaying/Neutering

Neutering a male dog or spaying a female dog is an important way to keep the dog healthy. Females spayed at a young age have almost no risk of developing mammary tumors or reproductive problems. An unspayed female is prone to mammary tumors and should have the areas around her nipples checked for lumps on a regular basis. These tumors are often cancerous and could shorten an otherwise healthy dog's life.

Neutering a male is a great solution to dog aggression and also removes the chances of testicular cancer. A male dog that has not been neutered should have his testicles checked regularly for the formation of tumors as well. This is especially important as the dog ages.

Female dogs usually experience their first heat cycle between 6 months and 1 year of age. Unless spayed they will continue to come into heat on a regular cycle. The length of time between heats varies, with anything from every six months to a year being normal.

There is absolutely no benefit to a female having a first season before being spayed, nor in letting her have a litter. Bitches do not have a physical or behavioral need to have puppies. Spaying a female dog relieves the

---

ADVANTAGES OF SPAY/NEUTER

The greatest advantage of spaying (for females) or neutering (for males) your dog is that you are guaranteed your dog will not produce puppies. There are too many puppies already available for too few homes. There are other advantages as well.

ADVANTAGES OF SPAYING

No messy heats.

No "suitors" howling at your windows or waiting in your yard.

Decreased incidences of pyometra (disease of the uterus) and breast cancer.

ADVANTAGES OF NEUTERING

Lessens male aggressive and territorial behaviors, but doesn't affect the dog's personality. Behaviors are often owner-induced, so neutering is not the only answer, but it is a good start.

Prevents the need to roam in search of bitches in season.

Decreased incidences of urogenital diseases.

owner from the worries involved with keeping her isolated during her heats, from unwanted litters and from the headaches associated with breeding puppies.

Many of the same considerations apply to choosing not to neuter a male Great Dane. They, too, must meet the same criteria for health and soundness if used to sire a litter. The owner of a male dog has no control over where the resulting puppies will be placed. However, when it comes to problems that may come up as those puppies grow to adulthood, the owner of the sire is just as responsible as the owner of the dam for the well-being of the offspring.

If a male dog shows signs of aggression toward other dogs, neutering will almost always alleviate the situation. Many unneutered male dogs howl, seek ways to escape and stop eating altogether when there is a female in heat nearby. A neutered male will not be affected by the presence of a female in season, whether she is in the house or just in the neighborhood. All in all he will be a more pleasant dog to live with.

The decision to breed any female dog should be well thought out. You need to ask yourself whether the dog is a good physical specimen of the breed. Is he in excellent health and does he have a sound temperament? There are several genetic problems associated with Great Danes—you must screen your dog for such conditions before making the decision to breed her. If your Great Dane has any genetic predisposition to disease, he should never be considered for breeding.

Another serious consideration is finding suitable homes for the puppies. Due to their great size, Danes must go to homes that are well prepared to care for this type of breed. Owning a dog is a lifetime commitment to that animal. There are so many unwanted dogs in shelters—even Great Danes—that people must be positively sure that they are not just adding to the pet overpopulation problem. Breeding a litter of puppies is not a sure way to make money. In fact, it is more likely that you will lose more than you will ever make when time, effort, equipment and veterinary costs are added up.

Should You Call the Veterinarian?

There will be times throughout your dog's life when you won't have a doubt about whether or not to take him to the veterinarian. There will be other times, however, when the decision will be less clear-cut. You should be aware of what is normal for your dog so that you have something to compare to when an abnormal situation arises. "Normal" includes energy, appetite, elimination patterns, appearance, pulse and temperature. Establish your dog's normal temperature at different times of the day to use as a guideline. **Only take your dog's temperature with a rectal thermometer.** Be sure to shake it down to 96°F and place a small amount of petroleum jelly on the tip prior to insertion. It is easiest to insert the thermometer while the dog is standing.

Lift up the tail and carefully insert the bulb end of the thermometer about 1½ inches into the anal opening. Don't let go, but leave it in for two to three minutes for the most accurate reading. The normal temperature range for a healthy adult dog is 100° to 102.5°F.

A dog's **pulse,** which measures the heartbeat, is taken by feeling the femoral artery, which is located in the groin region where the leg and body meet. The normal pulse for a healthy adult dog is 70 to 130 beats per minute. The rate will vary according to the size of the dog (puppies have faster heartbeats than adult dogs). A very athletic dog may have a slower pulse than average. Monitoring the temperature and pulse are important indicators of the dog's internal system and will help in determining illness or infection.

> ## WHEN TO CALL THE VET
>
> In any emergency situation, you should call your veterinarian immediately. You can make the difference in your dog's life by staying as calm as possible when you call and by giving the doctor or the assistant as much information as possible before you leave for the clinic. That way, the vet will be able to take immediate, specific action to remedy your dog's situation.
>
> Emergencies include acute abdominal pain, suspected poisoning, snakebite, burns, frostbite, shock, dehydration, abnormal vomiting or bleeding and deep wounds. You are the best judge of your dog's health, as you live with and observe him every day. Don't hesitate to call your veterinarian if you suspect trouble.

71

Some changes in your dog aren't as easy to determine. If your dog has a limp or his gait is off, there are many possibilities to consider. Obviously, if you see an injury occur, then you know the origin of your dog's problem. Assess the degree of severity of the injury to determine treatment. If your dog can't use a limb at all, you should suspect a break and take him to the veterinarian immediately. If the injury doesn't seem that acute but the dog is having problems walking and the limb or area in question is painful, swollen and feels warm to the touch, there may be an infection. Both need veterinary attention. Pulled muscles and sprains heal on their own, but the dog must be kept inactive so the area isn't stressed.

Lameness

If your dog begins limping for no apparent reason and it gets progressively worse, he has a potentially serious problem. First, try to assess where the problem actually is. Check the legs and feet for any tender, swollen or infected areas. There are many possibilities to consider. In young, developing dogs, lameness in the rear legs can be a symptom of hip dysplasia.

Hip dysplasia is a malformation of the ball and socket joint of the hips and can affect one or both sides of the dog. With age, these joints wear down, and eventually arthritis is associated with the disease. Hip dysplasia is properly diagnosed by x-ray.

If x-rays do confirm hip dysplasia, there are several options. In more serious cases, surgery is an alternative; the pectinius muscle can be split or the femoral head removed. In very severe cases the hips themselves are removed and replaced with Teflon hips. Dogs with very mild hip dysplasia may lead normal lives if properly managed. This type of dog must be kept at a good weight and in good physical condition. Moderate exercise, particularly swimming, is necessary if a dysplastic dog is to lead a normal life. If pain develops as the dog gets older, it can be relieved with aspirin.

Osteochondritis dissecans (OCD) is a disease that affects the shoulder joints and sometimes the hocks and stifles. It commonly causes lameness in young dogs. It is caused by faulty cartilage lining the ends of the long bones. As the dog exercises, the cartilage is damaged. OCD can be diagnosed by x-ray—the cartilage will appear fragmented or loose. In mild cases this will heal itself with rest, but usually OCD requires surgery.

A very serious concern with lameness, especially in older dogs, is **bone cancer.** This can only be diagnosed by tests and x-rays.

If your dog or puppy becomes lame and the veterinarian prescribes rest as treatment, the dog must be kept almost completely inactive except for bathroom time until the injury heals. Even a "short" walk will prolong the healing process. If your dog is extremely active, you may need to keep him in a crate in order to prevent reinjury and to promote healing.

Healthy Great Danes are in good physical condition and love to play.

Not Eating or Vomiting

One of the surest signs that a Great Dane may be ill is if he isn't eating. This is why it is important to know your dog's eating habits. For most dogs, one missed meal under normal conditions is not cause for alarm, but more than that and it is time to search for reasons. The vital signs should be checked and the gums examined. Normally a dog's gums are pink; if ill, they will be pale and gray.

If a lack of appetite has no other associated symptoms, it may be a sign of some form of cancer. Blood work done by a veterinarian is necessary for diagnosis. Poor appetite is also associated with kidney failure. Another indication that this may be occurring is increased water consumption and frequent urination. Dogs with kidney failure need special medication, an appetite booster and a special diet. An unspayed female with poor appetite and signs of lethargy may have pyometra, an infection of the uterus.

There are many reasons why dogs vomit, and many of them are not cause for alarm. If they eat too much grass, they vomit. If they drink too much water too quickly, they often vomit. If they eat something that does not agree with them, they get rid of it before it makes them more ill. A single occurrence of vomiting generally requires no action other than giving Pepto Bismol and feeding the dog a mild diet for a day or so.

You should be concerned when your dog vomits frequently over the period of a day. If the vomiting is associated with diarrhea, elevated temperature and lethargy, the cause is most likely a virus. The dog should receive supportive veterinary treatment if recovery is to proceed quickly.

Vomiting that is not associated with other symptoms is often an indication of an intestinal blockage. Considering the oral orientations of most dogs this can be a real concern. Rocks, toys and clothing will lodge in a dog's intestine, preventing the normal passage of digested foods and liquids. This is often difficult for a veterinarian to diagnose. Many times they will treat blockages as gastrointestinal disturbances for days until the dog becomes so weakened and dehydrated he dies.

If a blockage is suspected the first thing to do is an x-ray of the stomach and intestinal region. Sometimes objects will pass on their own, but usually surgical removal of the object is necessary.

Diarrhea

Diarrhea is characterized as very loose to watery stools that a dog has difficulty controlling. It can be caused by something as simple as changing diet, eating rich human food or having internal parasites.

First try to locate the source of the problem and make it inaccessible to the dog. Immediate relief is usually

First try to locate the source of the problem and make it inaccessible to the dog. Immediate relief is usually available by giving the dog a human intestinal relief medication such as Kaopectate or Pepto Bismol. Calculate the appropriate amount by considering the dog's weight and give the same amount that a human of that weight should take. Take the dog off his food for a day to allow the intestines to rest, then feed meals of cooked rice with bland ingredients added. Gradually add the dog's regular food back into his diet.

If worms are suspected as the cause, a stool sample should be examined by a veterinarian and treatment to rid the dog of the parasite should follow when the dog is back to normal. If allergies are suspected, a series of tests can be given to find the cause. This is especially likely if, after recovery and no other evidence of a cause exists, a dog returns to his former diet and the diarrhea recurs. If the diarrhea is bloody or has a more offensive odor than might be expected and is combined with vomiting and fever, it is most likely caused by a virus and requires immediate veterinary attention.

Bloat

Recent studies at Purdue University on the subject of bloat, or gastric dilatation volvulus, provide the frightening information that statistically 25 percent of Great Danes will bloat. Because bloat usually is fatal, all Dane owners should be aware of the signs.

The most common sign is distention of the abdomen, but it isn't *always* present. The dog will appear restless and will usually try to vomit, bringing up only foam. He may want to dig and may appear to be in great pain. If you even *suspect* that your dog might be in bloat, rush him to the vet or emergency clinic ASAP! You will have only about ½ an hour prior to irreparable damage or death. It's a good idea to discuss this possibility with your vet prior to facing the emergency.

What happens during bloat? The stomach fills with gas and, for some as yet unknown reason, cannot expel the gas. As it continues to fill, the stomach will often begin to rotate on its axis, thus occluding the nerves and blood vessels that service the stomach area. After a short time, the stomach wall will begin to die due to lack of blood/oxygen flow. Once this begins, the entire system can become septic, with heart involvement often becoming the immediate cause of death.

To date, the causes are still unknown. The Purdue study has suggested that dogs fed a diet full of variety and who have calmer dispositions are at a lesser risk. Feeding a minimum of 2 meals a day, waiting 1 hour before and after feeding to exercise, and perhaps soaking the food are also thought to be of some help in preventing bloat. The most effective preventative is a gastropexy. This is a surgical procedure where the stomach wall is securely attached to the abdominal wall. The adhesions formed after surgery further help to anchor the stomach so it cannot torsion. You should discuss this procedure with your vet. I routinely do a gastropexy on my adult bitches when they're spayed.

Seizures

Seizures are one of the most frightening occurrences a dog owner can witness. Seizures vary in severity from trembling and stiffness to frenzied, rapid movements of the legs, foaming at the mouth and loss of urine and bowel movements. The latter is usually considered a grand mal seizure.

Seizures are caused by electrical activity in the brain, and there are many reasons why they may occur. Ingestion of some poisons, such as strychnine and insecticides, will cause seizures. These are generally long-lasting and severe in nature. Blood tests often confirm the presence of poison and organ damage. Injuries to the skull, tumors and cancers can also trigger seizures. Diagnosis of the injury or presence of the disease is usually enough to confirm the cause.

Seizures vary in length and always seem longer than they actually are. Most first-time seizures that are not caused by poisonings will have a duration of up to two minutes. Typically the seizure will stop, and after a few minutes or even hours of disorientation, the dog returns to his normal behavior. Never try to touch or move a dog during a seizure. They may accidentally bite in this state. If there is anything nearby that might be knocked over by their flailing legs and injure them, move it out of the way. If the seizure does not stop within five minutes, call your veterinarian.

Even after a typical seizure, you may want to contact your veterinarian and discuss your options. Your veterinarian may suggest you bring your dog in for an examination and blood work. If a cause is not found, the best course is usually to wait and see if your dog has another seizure. If a dog has seizures once or twice a year there is no reason to place him on preventive medication.

If, however, there appears to be no reason for the seizure it is possible the cause is congenital epilepsy. In typical epilepsy, a dog is in a state of aura for as long as a day before the seizure occurs. The dog may act restless and stare and bark at things that do not exist. The seizure itself lasts several minutes. A second seizure can be triggered by turning a light on or moving the dog as he is recovering.

If seizures occur on a regular basis and are of the same nature each time, the dog is considered to have epilepsy and medication should be started. Commonly used drugs to prevent seizures include phenobarbital and Dilantin. The amount given will vary according to how much is needed to control frequent seizures.

If seizures are infrequent and mild, an epileptic dog can lead a fairly normal life. Owners will generally begin to see a pattern in the time of day and frequency the seizures occur, and can plan their dog's activities accordingly. Nonetheless, it is probably not a wise idea to subject a seizure-prone dog to excessive stress or exercise. The frequency and intensity of seizures often increase as time goes on, until the quality of the dog's life is questionable.

Coughing

Throughout the day many dogs will cough to get something out of their throats and it can usually be ignored. If coughing persists, then it is time to look for causes. Sometimes it is nothing more than grass seeds in the throat or a collar that is too tight.

A common cause for a dry, hacking cough is kennel cough, which is contagious and usually picked up through association with other dogs. A dog with kennel cough should receive veterinary attention and be placed on antibiotics and a cough suppressant. During treatment and recovery, the dog should be kept indoors and warm as much as possible. Kennel cough, if not cared for properly, can easily turn into pneumonia in cold conditions. Dogs should be isolated from other dogs until they have recovered.

Applying abdominal thrusts can save a choking dog.

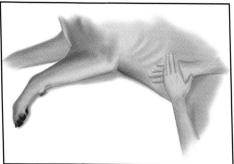

Coughing can also be a sign of heart failure, especially in an older dog after he has been exercised. It may also indicate a heartworm infection. If this occurs regularly, consult your veterinarian.

Most changes in the breathing pattern of a healthy dog, such as rapid inhalations or panting, are caused by exercise, stress and heat. The breathing pattern should return to normal in a short period of time.

If a dog is having problems breathing and it is also accompanied by coughing or gagging, it may be a sign that an air passage is blocked. Check for an object lodged in your dog's throat. If you can't remove it yourself, use the Heimlich maneuver. Place your dog on his side and, using both hands palms down, apply quick thrusts to the abdomen just below the dog's last rib. If your dog won't lie down, grasp either side of the end of the rib cage and squeeze in short thrusts. Make a sharp enough movement to cause the air in the lungs to force the object out. If the cause cannot be found or removed, then professional help is needed.

Shallow breathing can be a result of an injury to the ribs or a lung problem. A wheezing noise that can be heard as a dog breathes is an indication of a serious problem. If other symptoms include a fever and lethargy, the problem may be associated with a lung disease. If there is no fever, it may indicate heart disease or a lung tumor. The symptoms may indicate treatment for an infection, but an x-ray can confirm the presence of a growth or infection in the lungs.

Sometimes a dog exhibits no sign that something is different other than increased lethargy, weight gain or even a poor coat. It may be time to consider checking the dog's thyroid levels for a possible hypothyroid condition. Low thyroid most commonly results in a poor coat and skin and eventual infertility in an intact male or female. A thyroid test will indicate what levels of the function of the thyroid are low and whether daily thyroid medication should be given.

Skin Problems

Certain skin conditions should not be ignored if home treatment is not working. For example, if a dog is so sensitive and allergic to the saliva of a flea that his coat and skin are literally destroyed by chewing, it is time to seek help. Cortisone can help relieve the itching and stop the dog from destroying himself, but it has side effects, too! It's best to get your veterinarian's advice.

Mange is caused by a tiny mite that lives on the dog's skin. The most common types are sarcoptic and demodetic mange. While they can be treated without veterinary assistance, actual diagnosis may have to be by a veterinarian as the mites are too small to be seen.

Sarcoptic mange first appears as small red bumps on the dog's skin and causes intense itching. If allowed to continue, there is hair loss from chewing, and the affected skin becomes crusty.

*Run your
hands regularly
over your dog
to feel for any
injuries.*

The mite that causes demodetic mange lives in the pores of the skin of most dogs. Certain conditions cause the dog's natural immunity to this mite to break down, and the result is patches of hair loss, usually around the nose or eyes. There is no itching associated with this condition and it primarily occurs in dogs under 1 year of age. If treated properly, the hair returns to normal. In the generalized form of the disease, hair loss occurs in large patches all over the body.

Obviously this is a much more serious condition.

One of the most baffling skin problems is **hot spots.** They can be caused by a number of things—flea bites and allergies are common culprits. A warm, moist, infected area on the skin appears out of nowhere and can be several inches large. At home, one should clip the hair around it, then clean it with an antiseptic cleaning solution and dilute hydrogen peroxide. Topical ointments can also help. If the spot is not healing and appears to be getting larger or infected, veterinary help should be sought.

A similar type of skin condition is the **lick sore.** These sores are almost always on the lower part of the front legs or tops of the feet. Some dogs are more prone to develop these than others. A dog will lick a spot and out of boredom continue licking it until the hair is gone and the skin is hard, red and shiny. The sore will heal on its own if kept clean and the dog is prevented access to it by an antichewing spray or by wearing an Elizabethan collar.

Tumors

As dogs age they are more apt to develop various types of tumors. These may be sebaceous cysts, which appear as small bumps on or within the skin. They are usually harmless unless they become infected and begin to increase in size. Fatty tumors grow just under the dog's skin and are not attached to anything. These are usually benign accumulations of fatty cells. If you see or feel any such lumps on your dog, you should consult your veterinarian. Tumors and bumps that appear and grow rapidly, are strange in color or appearance or are attached to the bone should receive immediate attention.

Giving Medication

Anytime a dog has been diagnosed with a problem that requires medication, it is usually in the form of a pill or liquid.

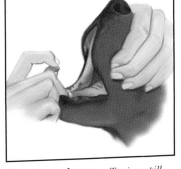

Because it is essential for a dog to have the entire pill or capsule in order for the dosage to be effective, it's necessary to actually give the dog the pill rather than mixing it in his food or wrapping it in meat, which can be chewed up and spit out. Open your dog's mouth and place the pill on the back of the middle of his tongue. Then hold his head up with his mouth held shut and stroke his throat. When the dog swallows, you can let go.

To give a pill, open the mouth wide, then drop it in the back of the throat.

Liquid medication is most easily given in a syringe. These are usually marked so the amount is accurately measured. Hold the dog's head upward at about 45°, open the mouth slightly and place the end of the syringe in the area in the back of the mouth between the cheek and rear molars. Hold your dog's mouth shut until he swallows.

Squeeze eye ointment into the lower lid.

If your dog needs eye medication, apply it by pulling down the lower eyelid and placing the ointment on the inside of the lid. Then close the eye and gently disperse the solution around the eye. Eye drops can be placed directly on the eye. Giving ear medicine is similar to cleaning the ears. The drops are placed in the canal and the ear is then massaged.

Cuts and Wounds

Lacerations of the skin most commonly occur from dogfights, though dogs have been known to do such things as go through a window after a cat or rabbit. Any cut over half an inch in length should be stitched for it to heal. Small cuts usually heal by themselves if they are rinsed well, washed with an antibiotic soap and

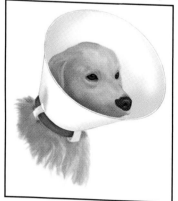

An Elizabethan collar keeps your dog from licking a fresh wound.

checked regularly with further cleansing of soap or a hydrogen peroxide solution. When they occur in areas that are exposed to dirt, such as the feet, it may be advisable to place a wrap on the injury, but it should be removed frequently. If signs of infection appear, such as swelling, redness and warmth, the wound should be looked at by a veterinarian.

Puncture wounds should never be bandaged or stitched. They occur most commonly from bites, nails or wires. Anytime it is suspected that a dog might have been pierced by a nail or bitten, the body should be carefully examined for such wounds. As they often do not bleed very much, they can be difficult to spot. If not treated, they can result in infection or even conditions as dangerous as tetanus.

Common Great Dane Problems

Large dogs like Great Danes are particularly susceptible to bloat, discussed earlier. Other afflictions commonly found in the breed follow.

Cardiomyopathy The most common cardiac problem that affects Great Danes, frequently males, is cardiomyopathy. The developing cardiomyopathy is usually undetected until severe symptoms occur. Sudden weight loss, lack of energy, exercise intolerance and abdominal distention are common. Clinical signs are atrial fibrillation and the heart ventricles are often grossly enlarged and flabby. The heart is no longer able to pump blood efficiently.

Cataracts Great Danes are usually affected by juvenile cataracts. They are characterized by the part of the lens on which they appear and the age of the dog. Most are genetic, though others can be caused by injury or the aging process. Most cataracts are nonprogressive in Danes and impairment of vision is usually mild. Diagnosis must be made by a veterinary ophthalmologist.

Cervical Vertebral Instability (CVI) or Wobblers Syndrome CVI is caused by an instability or malformation of the cervical spine (neck) vertebrae. The malformation puts pressure on the spinal cord and causes a lack of coordination (ataxia) in the rear legs. In severe cases, the forelegs are also affected, and in some cases the dog cannot walk at all. There is usually no pain associated with this disease. What actually causes the malformation is unknown although inheritance is a major suspect. CVI can also be brought on by injury. The usual age of onset in Great Danes is around 7 to 8 months of age, but it can occur much earlier.

If you know your dog well, you'll probably recognize when something's wrong with his health.

There is a surgical treatment for CVI in which the affected vertebrae are fused to each other, thus stabilizing this part of the spine. The problem that sometimes results is a malpositioning of the adjoining vertebrae due to increased stress. A veterinarian can determine if such surgery is necessary for an affected dog. In most cases, Great Danes with this problem are able to live long, happy lives with lots of good care and supervision.

Panosteoitis Panosteoitis, or "traveling lameness," is an inflammation of the long bones of the legs that can affect the growing puppy from 4 to 8 months of age. Typically, it will begin with a mild limp in one limb and then will migrate to another limb, affecting each limb in turn. During its active phases, it can be diagnosed via x-ray. Panosteoitis is self-limiting, usually disappearing by the age of 1 year.

There is usually not a lot of pain associated with this condition, but if there is, your vet can prescribe an anti-inflammatory medication to ease your puppy's discomfort. The cause of panosteoitis is unknown, and there is no medical cure other than time.

von Willebrands Disease   This disease is a genetic bleeding disorder that might be suspected if it takes longer than normal for a wound to stop bleeding. Other indications are high mortality rates in newborn puppies or poor fertility in a female. A blood specimen treated and tested at a specially equipped facility is necessary to diagnose this disease.

Cropping Ears

Canada and the United States remain among the few countries where ear cropping is still allowed. Some breeders crop their puppies ears before offering them for adoption and others leave the decision up to the new owners. If you are trying to decide whether to crop your Great Dane's ears, it is important to learn the advantages and disadvantages of cropping.

The uncropped ear presents several problems for Great Danes. Uncropped ears tend to form hematomas at the end of the ear, which occurs when the head is shaken hard. The ear tips snap against the ear, similar to a snapped dish towel, and often the blood vessels will break and bleed into the surrounding tissue. What you will then see is a swelling at the site where the blood vessels have broken. Not only is this painful to the dog, but it's not uncommon for the inflamed area to break open the next time the dog shakes his head.

Infection is also more likely to occur in an uncropped ear than a cropped one. However, infections are not common because the ear canal in a Dane is large and open, even when the ear flap covers it.

Many people prefer the look of a Dane with cropped ears, but don't realize the effort it will take on their part to train the ears to stand properly. Having a Dane with lovely, erect ears takes much more diligence than simply having them cropped by a knowledgeable veterinarian. If your puppy's ears aren't cropped at the time you purchase him, you cannot simply take him to any veterinarian and ask to have the ears cropped. You will need to find a veterinarian who has knowledge of the correct procedure, has lots of experience performing it and knows how to provide the right care after cropping. Puppies cropped by veterinarians who have a great deal of experience and expertise in this field usually come out of the anesthetic ready to romp and play. There should be little or no pain unless they scratch at the ears or get bumped by a littermate. Ask your puppy's breeder for recommendations of qualified veterinarians for this procedure.

Training cropped ears to stand erect takes a lot of time, diligence and patience.

AFTER-CARE FOR CROPPED EARS

There are many after-care methods for cropped ears. In some methods, the ear and the ear canal are completely enclosed, and in others, the ears are left open to the air. I much prefer and recommend any method that leaves the ears open. The open-air method diminishes the likelihood of irritation and infections. Ask the veterinarian or the puppy's breeder to give you a lesson and take-home instructions for taping and bracing cropped ears. The best way to ensure beautifully cropped ears is to be diligent about taping them and assess for any signs of infection or discomfort to the puppy.

When your puppy comes home after being cropped, he'll either have his ears taped to a wire rack that holds the ears erect, or he'll have his ears taped to a brace made out of Styrofoam cups. He'll wear this appliance for approximately ten days to two weeks. The stitches should be taken out around this same time by the veterinarian who cropped the pup's ears.

Once the stitches are out, the ears need to be trained to stay erect—they aren't going to learn to stand unless you help them along. This is where the taping comes in. The veterinarian or breeder can do this for you the first time and show you how to reapply the tape. It's a detailed and involved procedure that must be learned correctly over time. Ear taping usually continues until the puppy is 5 or 6 months old. Ideally the ears stay up in training tapes and braces for two weeks at a time. Then they are removed, the ears are allowed to flop and rest for a few days and then back up they go. Many people unfamiliar with Great Danes are not given the details of this process before having their pup's ears cropped. Now that you're armed with the facts, you can make an informed choice to crop, or not to crop.

A FIRST-AID KIT

Keep a canine first-aid kit on hand for general care and emergencies. Check it periodically to make sure liquids haven't spilled or dried up, and replace medications and materials after they're used. Your kit should include:

Activated charcoal tablets

Adhesive tape
(1 and 2 inches wide)

Antibacterial ointment
(for skin and eyes)

Aspirin (buffered or enteric coated, *not* Ibuprofen)

Bandages: Gauze rolls (1 and 2 inches wide) and dressing pads

Cotton balls

Diarrhea medicine

Dosing syringe

Hydrogen peroxide (3%)

Petroleum jelly

Rectal thermometer

Rubber gloves

Rubbing alcohol

Scissors

Tourniquet

Towel

Tweezers

First Aid and Emergencies

When a veterinarian is not immediately available, first-aid measures can be taken to help ensure that your dog's condition is stabilized. Anytime a dog is in extreme pain, even the most docile one may bite if touched. As a precaution, the dog's mouth should be restrained with some type of **muzzle.** A rope, pair of pantyhose or strip of cloth about 2 feet long all work in a pinch.

First tie a loose knot that has an opening large enough to easily fit around the dog's nose. Once it is on, tighten the knot on the top of the muzzle. Then bring the two ends down and tie another knot underneath the dog's chin. Finally, pull the ends behind the head and tie a knot below the ears. Don't do this if there is an injury to the head or the dog requires artificial respiration.

Use a scarf or old hose to make a temporary muzzle, as shown.

Artificial respiration is necessary if breathing has stopped. Situations that may cause a state of unconsciousness include drowning, choking, electric shock or even shock itself. If you've taken a course in human CPR, you will discover that similar methods are used on dogs. The first thing to do is check the mouth and air passages for any object that might obstruct breathing. If you find nothing, or when it is cleared, hold the dog's mouth while covering the nose completely with your mouth. Gently exhale into the dog's nose. This should be done at between ten to twelve breaths per minute.

If the heart has stopped beating, place the dog on his right side and place the palm of your hand on the rib cage just behind the elbows. Press down six times and then wait five seconds and repeat. This should be done in conjunction with artificial respiration, so it will require two people. Artificial respiration should be continued until the dog breathes on his own. Heart massage should continue until the heart beats on its own.

If a dog has been injured or is too ill to walk on his own, he will have to be carried to be moved. It is important to be very careful when this is done to prevent further injury or trauma. Keep the dog's body as flat and still as possible. Two people are usually needed to move a large dog. A blanket can work if all four corners are held taut. A piece of plywood or extremely stiff cardboard works best, if available.

Whenever a dog is injured or is seriously ill the odds are good that it will go into a state of **shock.** A dog in shock will be listless, weak and cold to the touch. His gums will be pale. If not treated a dog will die from shock even if the illness or injuries themselves are not fatal. The conditions of the dog should continue to be treated, but the dog should be kept as comfortable as possible. A blanket can help keep the dog warm. A dog in shock needs immediate veterinary care.

Make a temporary splint by wrapping the leg in firm casing, then bandaging it.

When **severe bleeding** from a cut occurs the area should be covered with bandaging material or a clean cloth and should have pressure applied to it. If it appears that an artery is involved and the wound is on a limb, then a tourniquet should be applied. This can be made of a piece of cloth, gauze or sock if nothing else is available. It should be tied above the wound and checked every few minutes to make sure it is not so tight that circulation to the rest of the limb is cut off.

If a **fracture** is felt or suspected, the dog should be moved and transported as carefully as possible to a veterinarian. Attempting to treat a break at home can cause more damage than leaving it alone.

In the case of **poisoning,** the only thing to do is get help immediately. If you know the source of the poison, take the container or object with you to the clinic as this may aid treatment. If a dog ingests a petroleum product, vegetable or mineral oil can be given for the gastrointestinal tract at a dosage of 1 tablespoon per 5 pounds of weight.

Some of the household substances harmful to your dog.

In acidic or alkaline poisonings, the chemicals must be neutralized. Pepto Bismol or milk of magnesia at 2 teaspoons per 5 pounds can be given for acids. Vinegar diluted at one part to four parts water at the same dosage can relieve alkaline poisons.

Heatstroke

Heatstroke occurs when a dog's body temperature greatly exceeds the normal 101.5°F. It can be caused by overexertion in warm temperatures, or if a dog is left in a closed vehicle for any period of time. A dog should *never* be left in an unventilated, unshaded vehicle. Even if you only plan to be gone for a minute, that time can unexpectedly increase and place a dog in a life-threatening situation.

Dogs suffering from heatstroke will feel hot to the touch and inhale short, shallow, rapid breaths. The heartbeat will be very fast. The dog must be cooled immediately, preferably being wet down with cool water in any way that is available. The dog should be wrapped in cool, damp towels. Shock is another possible side effect of heatstroke. The dog should also receive veterinary care. Even when a dog survives heatstroke, permanent damage often occurs.

The opposite of heatstroke is **hypothermia.** When a dog is exposed to extreme cold for long periods of time, his body temperature drops, he becomes chilled and can go into shock. The dog should be placed in a warm environment and wrapped in towels or blankets. If the dog is already wet, a warm bath can help. Massaging the body will help increase the circulation to normal levels.

Insect Bites

The seriousness of reactions to insect bites varies. The affected area will be red, swollen and painful. In the case of bee stings, the stinger should always be removed. A paste made of baking soda can be applied to the wound and ice applied to the area for the relief of swelling. The bites of some spiders, centipedes and scorpions can cause severe illness and lead to shock.

Porcupines

If a dog has an encounter with a porcupine, those quills will need to be removed. The quill should be grasped with a pair of pliers in the area just above the dog's skin. A quick tug should remove it. If a quill breaks off and is left in the skin, it will need to be removed by a veterinarian. If left in, the quills can migrate through the dog's body and cause infection.

Skunks

If your dog is sprayed by a skunk, he will not require veterinary attention, but he will be unbearable to live with. Getting rid of the odor is not easy, despite all of the remedies in the world. Several products are available specifically for skunk-odor removal. If you can't find or buy one in time, plain old vinegar can work, as can mixtures of baking soda and hydrogen peroxide, or good old tomato juice. Some people find feminine douche preparations effective.

Despite what one decides to use, the dog will need to be thoroughly wet down. The solution is then applied to the dog's coat and allowed to sit for ten minutes (or whatever the directions recommend). Even after being rinsed off with clear water, the odor often remains. Repeating the process several times is often necessary.

A faint skunk odor may linger for some time even after the most thorough de-skunking sessions.

Care of the Older Dog

Sometime down the line, your charming, always-getting-into-trouble puppy will become your canine senior citizen, so it's in your Great Dane's best interest to consider the senior years.

It is commonly felt by most Great Dane breeders that every year after six is a grace period. It is then that you need to develop a more vigilant eye and make changes as your Great Dane ages, to make his days more comfortable and enjoyable.

Like us, they end where they began—sleeping more, needing to go out more, forgetting sometimes where they were heading and why, wanting to eat more often and very much needing reassurance and the security of our love.

It is easy to become impatient with our old-timers. They can be demanding. They want what they want *now.* Just a few suggestions:

Sometimes bringing in a younger companion will add years to an old-timer's life. Not a very young puppy but one old enough to have lost the sharp puppy teeth and have some sense—a 4- or 5-month-old Great Dane can still be molded into a fine companion, not taking as much time as an 8- to 12-week-old puppy but offering your old-timer some companionship.

You shouldn't do it if your senior is over 7, but when he's 5 or 6, the introduction should not be too traumatic. But, there are exceptions. In one case, a year-old Great Dane, Jenny, left to go live with her 5-year-old-mother and Davey, who was over 8. There were no problems, and the "old man" adjusted marvelously well. The ironic part here was that Jenny had been sold to Davey's owners when she was barely 6 weeks old, but one of the reasons why they left her with her breeder was that they were concerned about the older dog and thought a young puppy would be too much. In the back of the breeders' minds was the reality that Davey would not be with them much longer! Jenny, however, is a pensive, gentle dog, and the "old man" has perked up!

One breeder wonders if her seniors live so long because her dogs are all house dogs and range in age from 5-week-old litters, kept in the kitchen, to the matriarch or patriarch of the house. The youngsters keep life lively and interesting and coax the seniors into more outside time and even an occasional romp.

You must never put your old-timer's nose out of joint, however, by cutting back on his time. If anything, give him more individual attention.

A younger dog can act as ears and eyes for a Great Dane losing his hearing or forming cataracts and even one who is blind. They sense the needs of their not-so-spry companion and help as they can. (The Great Dane is such a delight to live with that most people always want another one as a companion for the one they have lived with for a year or so.) Older dogs often become insecure when noise or unfamiliar situations startle them. A pair of younger ears to sound an alarm reassures them.

You'll notice as your dog ages that you will be able to leave the room and even the house without disturbing him! You'll also be able to come into the house and find him still sleeping, snoring contentedly. It is a lonely feeling not to be greeted at the door, and perhaps to prepare for that, you may want to bring in another dog when your Great Dane is 5 or 6. You'll have an age gap that will be comfortable, and you won't feel that the younger dog is a replacement for the one you lose because he's been there and has been his own "person" and will have his *own* name. It is not recommended that you name your second dog after your first. (This won't happen, of course, if your first Dane is still with you.)

Remember, old dogs can sometimes be crotchety and demanding, and they don't like changes in their routine, though they adapt. And they snore! But, they are also dignified and still very much the loving dog they always were—they just show it in different ways, and when you look into their eyes, clouded by time, they look back at you with such patience and such wisdom and such dignity. And so much love!

Make sure you have periodical checks of stool, urine and teeth so you can keep your oldster comfortable. See if your veterinarian recommends a senior diet or one specific to your dog's physical needs or problems.

Make sure he is warm where he sleeps and free from drafts, and make allowances for his fading eyesight and his not-too-keen hearing. At some point, he will no longer be pretending not to hear you.

Always leave a light on in the kitchen and make sure there is a light on when he goes out in the dark. You should also be aware of how your oldster handles any stairs or steps and help him accordingly.

If you walk him, keep the pace moderate and cut the distance down gradually. Try to stop before he tires; remember, he also has to walk back to the house.

Feed smaller meals more often because sometimes they forget they ate and will drive you crazy!

Cover their favorite sleeping place with a mattress pad that has a rubber side, and so, if they have an accident during the night or in the daytime when you're not there, it won't soil their bedding or the chair.

Saying Good-Bye

The last thing you have to do is the hardest—knowing when to let go. Your heart won't like it, but your head has to rule here. Hopefully, all of them will die peacefully in their sleep, but we know that's not reality. One owner reports that of all the dogs she had, only one went that way. And she really didn't die in her sleep, because the owners had put her in her open crate while she dressed hurriedly to take her to the veterinarian. When the owner got back to her, the dog had slipped away. Should that happen to your Great Dane—that he slip away while you are not there or are asleep—have a friend help you gather him up wrapped in a blanket and take him to the veterinarian. Knowing ahead of time what to do with him makes it easier.

Some pet owners prefer to bury their dogs, some prefer to do something in honor of their beloved pets. For example, you can plant a tree in your dog's name. Or you may prefer to save the ashes of your soulmate. All dogs are dear to their owners, but a particular dog may hold a special place in your heart. You may not imagine that you can handle your dog's death, but you will, and you may be comfortable having his ashes in a container in the house. You may eventually want to remember your dog by doing something with the ashes, or you may simply find peace in keeping the ashes close to you.

Please remember that it is the *quality* of your Great Dane's life that's important, and when pain and lack of dignity take that quality away, we have to make a decision. If we don't, we're keeping them alive for us, and that is selfish. Remember them as light and sunshine, but when they become darkness, and suffering takes away their delight in life, it's time. Your head will know that you are doing the right thing for your dog. Your veterinarian will not make the decision for you. You have to read between the lines of what he's telling you and keep your heart quiet while you make the best decision for your dog.

Your Happy, Healthy Pet

Your Dog's Name _____

Name on Your Dog's Pedigree (if your dog has one) _____

_____

Where Your Dog Came From _____

_____

Your Dog's Birthday _____

Your Dog's Veterinarian

    Name _____

    Address _____

    Phone Number_____

    Emergency Number_____

Your Dog's Health

    Vaccines

    type _____ date given _____

    type _____ date given _____

    type _____ date given _____

    type _____ date given _____

    Heartworm

    date tested _____ type used_____ start date _____

Your Dog's License Number_____

Groomer's Name and Number _____

Dogsitter/Walker's Name and Number_____

Awards Your Dog Has Won

    Award _____ date earned _____

    Award _____ date earned _____

part three

Enjoying

your

Dog

chapter 8

Basic
Training

by Ian Dunbar, Ph.D., MRCVS

Training is the jewel in the crown—the most important aspect of doggy husbandry. There is no more important variable influencing dog behavior and temperament than the dog's education: A well-trained, well-behaved and good-natured puppydog is always a joy to live with, but an untrained and uncivilized dog can be a perpetual nightmare. Moreover, deny the dog an education and she will not have the opportunity to fulfill her own canine potential; neither will she have the ability to communicate effectively with her human companions.

Luckily, modern psychological training methods are easy, efficient, effective and, above all, considerably dog-friendly and user-friendly.

Doggy education is as simple as it is enjoyable. But before you can have a good time play-training with your new dog, you have to learn what to do and how to do it. There is no bigger variable influencing the success of dog training than the *owner's* experience and expertise. *Before you embark on the dog's education, you must first educate yourself.*

Basic Training for Owners

Ideally, basic owner training should begin well *before* you select your dog. Find out all you can about your chosen breed first, then master rudimentary training and handling skills. If you already have your puppy-dog, owner training is a dire emergency—the clock is ticking! Especially for puppies, the first few weeks at home are the most important and influential days in the dog's life. Indeed, the cause of most adolescent and adult problems may be traced back to the initial days the pup explores her new home. This is the time to establish the *status quo*—to teach the puppydog how you would like her to behave and so prevent otherwise quite predictable problems.

In addition to consulting breeders and breed books such as this one (which understandably have a positive breed bias), seek out as many pet owners with your breed as you can find. Good points are obvious. What you want to find out are the breed-specific *problems,* so you can nip them in the bud. In particular, you should talk to owners with *adolescent* dogs and make a list of all anticipated problems. Most important, *test drive* at least half a dozen adolescent and adult dogs of your breed yourself. An 8-week-old puppy is deceptively easy to handle, but she will acquire adult size, speed and strength in just four months, so you should learn now what to prepare for.

Puppy and pet dog training classes offer a convenient venue to locate pet owners and observe dogs in action. For a list of suitable trainers in your area, contact the Association of Pet Dog Trainers (see chapter 13). You may also begin your basic owner training by observing other owners in class. Watch as many classes and test drive as many dogs as possible. Select an upbeat, dog-friendly, people-friendly, fun-and-games, puppydog pet training class to learn the ropes. Also, watch training videos and read training books. You must find out what to do and how to do it *before* you have to do it.

Principles of Training

Most people think training comprises teaching the dog to do things such as sit, speak and roll over, but even a 4-week-old pup knows how to do these things already. Instead, the first step in training involves teaching the dog human words for each dog behavior and activity and for each aspect of the dog's environment. That way you, the owner, can more easily participate in the dog's domestic education by directing her to perform specific actions appropriately, that is, at the right time, in the right place and so on. Training opens communication channels, enabling an educated dog to at least understand her owner's requests.

In addition to teaching a dog *what* we want her to do, it is also necessary to teach her *why* she should do what we ask. Indeed, 95 percent of training revolves around motivating the dog *to want to do* what we want. Dogs often understand what their owners want; they just don't see the point of doing it—especially when the owner's repetitively boring and seemingly senseless instructions are totally at odds with much more pressing and exciting doggy distractions. It is not so much the dog that is being stubborn or dominant; rather, it is the owner who has failed to acknowledge the dog's needs and feelings and to approach training from the dog's point of view.

THE MEANING OF INSTRUCTIONS

The secret to successful training is learning how to use training lures to predict or prompt specific behaviors—to coax the dog to do what you want *when* you want. Any highly valued object (such as a treat or toy) may be used as a lure, which the dog will follow with her eyes and nose. Moving the lure in specific ways entices the dog to move her nose, head and entire body in specific ways. In fact, by learning the art of manipulating various lures, it is possible to teach the dog to assume virtually any body position and perform any action. Once you have control over the expression of the dog's behaviors and can elicit any body position or behavior at will, you can easily teach the dog to perform on request.

Teach your dog words for each activity she needs to know, like down.

Tell your dog what you want her to do, use a lure to entice her to respond correctly, then profusely praise and maybe reward her once she performs the desired action. For example, verbally request "Tina, sit!" while you move a squeaky toy upwards and backwards over the dog's muzzle (lure-movement and hand signal), smile knowingly as she looks up (to follow the lure) and sits down (as a result of canine anatomical engineering), then praise her to distraction ("Gooood Tina!"). Squeak the toy, offer a training treat and give your dog and yourself a pat on the back.

Being able to elicit desired responses over and over enables the owner to reward the dog over and over. Consequently, the dog begins to think training is fun. For example, the more the dog is rewarded for sitting, the more she enjoys sitting. Eventually the dog comes to realize that, whereas most sitting is appreciated, sitting immediately upon request usually prompts especially enthusiastic praise and a slew of high-level rewards. The dog begins to sit on cue much of the time, showing that she is starting to grasp the meaning of the owner's verbal request and hand signal.

WHY COMPLY?

Most dogs enjoy initial lure-reward training and are only too happy to comply with their owners' wishes. Unfortunately, repetitive drilling without appreciative feedback tends to diminish the dog's enthusiasm until she eventually fails to see the point of complying anymore. Moreover, as the dog approaches adolescence she becomes more easily distracted as she develops other interests. Lengthy sessions with repetitive exercises tend to bore and demotivate both parties. If it's not fun, the owner doesn't do it and neither does the dog.

Integrate training into your dog's life: The greater number of training sessions each day and the *shorter* they are, the more willingly compliant your dog will

become. Make sure to have a short (just a few seconds) training interlude before every enjoyable canine activity. For example, ask your dog to sit to greet people, to sit before you throw her Frisbee and to sit for her supper. Really, sitting is no different from a canine "Please."

To train your dog, you need gentle hands, a loving heart and a good attitude.

Also, include numerous short training interludes during every enjoyable canine pastime, for example, when playing with the dog or when she is running in the park. In this fashion, doggy distractions may be effectively converted into rewards for training. Just as all games have rules, fun becomes training . . . and training becomes fun.

Eventually, rewards actually become unnecessary to continue motivating your dog. If trained with consideration and kindness, performing the desired behaviors will become self-rewarding and, in a sense, your dog will motivate herself. Just as it is not necessary to reward a human companion during an enjoyable walk in the park, or following a game of tennis, it is hardly necessary to reward our best friend—the dog—for walking by our side or while playing fetch. Human company during enjoyable activities is reward enough for most dogs.

Even though your dog has become self-motivating, it's still good to praise and pet her a lot and offer rewards once in a while, especially for a good job well done. And if for no other reason, praising and rewarding others is good for the human heart.

PUNISHMENT

Without a doubt, lure-reward training is by far the best way to teach: Entice your dog to do what you want and then reward her for doing so. Unfortunately, a human shortcoming is to take the good for granted and to moan and groan at the bad. Specifically, the dog's many good behaviors are ignored while the owner focuses on punishing the dog for making mistakes. In extreme cases, instruction is *limited* to punishing mistakes made by a trainee dog, child, employee or husband, even though it has been proven punishment training is notoriously inefficient and ineffective and is decidedly unfriendly and combative. It teaches the dog that training is a drag, almost as quickly as it teaches the dog to dislike her trainer. Why treat our best friends like our worst enemies?

Punishment training is also much more laborious and time consuming. Whereas it takes only a finite amount of time to teach a dog what to chew, for example, it takes much, much longer to punish the dog for each and every mistake. Remember, *there is only one right way!* So why not teach that right way from the outset?!

103

To make matters worse, punishment training causes severe lapses in the dog's reliability. Since it is obviously impossible to punish the dog each and every time she misbehaves, the dog quickly learns to distinguish between those times when she must comply (so as to avoid impending punishment) and those times when she need not comply, because punishment is impossible. Such times include when the dog is off leash and 6 feet away, when the owner is otherwise engaged (talking to a friend, watching television, taking a shower, tending to the baby or chatting on the telephone) or when the dog is left at home alone.

Instances of misbehavior will be numerous when the owner is away, because even when the dog complied in the owner's looming presence, she did so unwillingly. The dog was forced to act against her will, rather than molding her will to want to please. Hence, when the owner is absent, not only does the dog know she need not comply, she simply does not want to. Again, the trainee is not a stubborn vindictive beast, but rather the trainer has failed to teach. Punishment training invariably creates unpredictable Jekyll and Hyde behavior.

Trainer's Tools

Many training books extol the virtues of a vast array of training paraphernalia and electronic and metallic gizmos, most of which are designed for canine restraint, correction and punishment, rather than for actual facilitation of doggy education. In reality, most effective training tools are not found in stores; they come from within ourselves. In addition to a willing dog, all you really need is a functional human brain, gentle hands, a loving heart and a good attitude.

In terms of equipment, all dogs do require a quality buckle collar to sport dog tags and to attach the leash (for safety and to comply with local leash laws). Hollow chew toys (like Kongs or sterilized longbones) and a dog bed or collapsible crate are musts for housetraining. Three additional tools are required:

1. specific lures (training treats and toys) to predict and prompt specific desired behaviors;

2. rewards (praise, affection, training treats and toys) to reinforce for the dog what a lot of fun it all is; and

3. knowledge—how to convert the dog's favorite activities and games (potential distractions to training) into "life-rewards," which may be employed to facilitate training.

The most powerful of these is *knowledge*. Education is the key! Watch training classes, participate in training classes, watch videos, read books, enjoy play-training with your dog and then your dog will say "Please," and your dog will say "Thank you!"

Housetraining

If dogs were left to their own devices, certainly they would chew, dig and bark for entertainment and then no doubt highlight a few areas of their living space with sprinkles of urine, in much the same way we decorate by hanging pictures. Consequently, when we ask a dog to live with us, we must teach her *where* she may dig, *where* she may perform her toilet duties, *what* she may chew and *when* she may bark. After all, when left at home alone for many hours, we cannot expect the dog to amuse herself by completing crosswords or watching the soaps on TV!

Also, it would be decidedly unfair to keep the house rules a secret from the dog, and then get angry and punish the poor critter for inevitably transgressing rules she did not even know existed. Remember: Without adequate education and guidance, the dog will be forced to establish her own rules—doggy rules—and most probably will be at odds with the owner's view of domestic living.

Since most problems develop during the first few days the dog is at home, prospective dog owners must be certain they are quite clear about the principles of housetraining *before* they get a dog. Early misbehaviors quickly become established as the *status quo*—

becoming firmly entrenched as hard-to-break bad habits, which set the precedent for years to come. Make sure to teach your dog good habits right from the start. Good habits are just as hard to break as bad ones!

Ideally, when a new dog comes home, try to arrange for someone to be present as much as possible during the first few days (for adult dogs) or weeks for puppies. With only a little forethought, it is surprisingly easy to find a puppy sitter, such as a retired person, who would be willing to eat from your refrigerator and watch your television while keeping an eye on the newcomer to encourage the dog to play with chew toys and to ensure she goes outside on a regular basis.

POTTY TRAINING

To teach the dog where to relieve herself:

1. never let her make a single mistake;
2. let her know where you want her to go; and
3. handsomely reward her for doing so: "GOOOOOOOD DOG!!!" liver treat, liver treat, liver treat!

Preventing Mistakes

A single mistake is a training disaster, since it heralds many more in future weeks. And each time the dog soils the house, this further reinforces the dog's unfortunate preference for an indoor, carpeted toilet. *Do not let an unhousetrained dog have full run of the house.*

When you are away from home, or cannot pay full attention, confine the dog to an area where elimination is appropriate, such as an outdoor run or, better still, a small, comfortable indoor kennel with access to an outdoor run. When confined in this manner, most dogs will naturally housetrain themselves.

If that's not possible, confine the dog to an area, such as a utility room, kitchen, basement or garage, where elimination may not be desired in the long run but as an interim measure it is certainly preferable to doing it all around the house. Use newspaper to cover the floor of the dog's day room. The newspaper may be used to soak up the urine and to wrap up and dispose of the feces. Once your dog develops a preferred spot for eliminating, it is only necessary to cover that part of the floor with newspaper. The smaller papered area may then be moved (only a little each day) towards the door to the outside. Thus the dog will develop the tendency to go to the door when she needs to relieve herself.

Never confine an unhousetrained dog to a crate for long periods. Doing so would force the dog to soil the crate and ruin its usefulness as an aid for housetraining (see the following discussion).

Teaching Where

In order to teach your dog where you would like her to do her business, you have to be there to direct the proceedings—an obvious, yet often neglected, fact of life. In order to be there to teach the dog *where* to go, you need to know *when* she needs to go. Indeed, the success of housetraining depends on the owner's ability to predict these times. Certainly, a regular feeding schedule will facilitate prediction somewhat, but there is nothing like "loading the deck" and influencing the timing of the outcome yourself!

The first few weeks at home are the most important and influential in your dog's life.

Whenever you are at home, make sure the dog is under constant supervision and/or confined to a small area. If already well trained, simply instruct the dog to lie down in her bed or basket. Alternatively, confine the dog to a crate (doggy den) or tie-down (a short, 18-inch lead that can be clipped to an eye hook in the baseboard near her bed). Short-term close confinement strongly inhibits urination and defecation, since the dog does not want to soil her sleeping area. Thus, when you release the puppydog each hour, she will definitely need to urinate immediately and defecate every third or fourth hour. Keep the dog confined to her doggy den and take her to her intended toilet area each hour, every hour and on the hour.

When taking your dog outside, instruct her to sit quietly before opening the door—she will soon learn to sit by the door when she needs to go out!

Teaching Why

Being able to predict when the dog needs to go enables the owner to be on the spot to praise and reward the dog. Each hour, hurry the dog to the intended toilet area in the yard, issue the appropriate instruction ("Go pee!" or "Go poop!"), then give the dog three to four minutes to produce. Praise and offer a couple of training treats when successful. The treats are important because many people fail to praise their dogs with feeling . . . and housetraining is hardly the time for understatement. So either loosen up and enthusiastically praise that dog: "Wuzzzer-wuzzer-wuzzer, hoooser good wuffer den? Hoooo went pee for Daddy?" Or say "Good dog!" as best you can and offer the treats for effect.

Following elimination is an ideal time for a spot of play-training in the yard or house. Also, an empty dog may be allowed greater freedom around the house for the next half hour or so, just as long as you keep an eye out to make sure she does not get into other kinds of mischief. If you are preoccupied and cannot pay full attention, confine the dog to her doggy den once more to enjoy a peaceful snooze or to play with her many chew toys.

If your dog does not eliminate within the allotted time outside—no biggie! Back to her doggy den, and then try again after another hour.

As I own large dogs, I always feel more relaxed walking an empty dog, knowing that I will not need to finish our stroll weighted down with bags of feces!

Beware of falling into the trap of walking the dog to get her to eliminate. The good ol' dog walk is such an enormous highlight in the dog's life that it represents the single biggest potential reward in domestic dogdom. However, when in a hurry, or during inclement weather, many owners abruptly terminate the walk the moment the dog has done her business. This, in effect, severely punishes the dog for doing the right thing, in the right place at the right time. Consequently, many dogs become strongly inhibited from eliminating outdoors because they know it will signal an abrupt end to an otherwise thoroughly enjoyable walk.

Instead, instruct the dog to relieve herself in the yard prior to going for a walk. If you follow the above instructions, most dogs soon learn to eliminate on cue. As soon as the dog eliminates, praise (and offer a treat or two)—"Good dog! Let's go walkies!" Use the walk as a reward for eliminating in the yard. If the dog does not go, put her back in her doggy den and think about a walk later on. You will find with a "No feces—no walk" policy, your dog will become one of the fastest defecators in the business.

If you do not have a backyard, instruct the dog to eliminate right outside your front door prior to the walk. Not only will this facilitate clean up and disposal of the feces in your own trash can but, also, the walk may again be used as a colossal reward.

CHEWING AND BARKING

Short-term close confinement also teaches the dog that occasional quiet moments are a reality of domestic living. Your puppydog is extremely impressionable during her first few weeks at home. Regular confinement at this time soon exerts a calming influ-ence over the dog's personality. Remember, once the dog is housetrained and calmer, there will be a whole lifetime ahead for the dog to enjoy full run of the house and garden. On the other hand, by letting the newcomer have unrestricted access to the entire house-hold and allowing her to run willy-nilly, she will most certainly develop a bunch of behavior problems in short order, no doubt necessitating confinement later in life. It would not be fair to remedially restrain and confine a dog you have trained, through neglect, to run free.

When confining the dog, make sure she always has an impressive array of suitable chew toys. Kongs and ster-ilized longbones (both readily available from pet stores) make the best chew toys, since they are hollow and may be stuffed with treats to heighten the dog's interest. For example, by stuffing the little hole at the top of a Kong with a small piece of freeze-dried liver, the dog will not want to leave it alone.

Remember, treats do not have to be junk food and they certainly should not represent extra calories. Rather, treats should be part of each dog's regular daily diet: Some food

may be served in the dog's bowl for break-fast and dinner, some food may be used as training treats, and some food may be used for stuffing chew toys. I regularly stuff my dogs' many Kongs with different shaped biscuits and kibble.

Make sure your puppy has suit-able chew toys.

The kibble seems to fall out fairly easily, as do the oval-shaped biscuits, thus rewarding the dog instanta-neously for checking out the chew toys. The bone-shaped biscuits fall out after a while, rewarding the dog for worrying at the chew toy. But the triangular biscuits never come out. They remain inside the Kong as lures, maintaining the dog's fascination with her chew toy. To further focus the dog's interest, I always make sure to flavor the triangular biscuits by rubbing them with a little cheese or freeze-dried liver.

To teach come, call your dog, open your arms as a welcoming signal, wave a toy or a treat and praise for every step in your direction.

If stuffed chew toys are reserved especially for times the dog is confined, the puppydog will soon learn to enjoy quiet moments in her doggy den and she will quickly develop a chew-toy habit— a good habit! This is a simple *autoshaping* process; all the owner has to do is set up the situation and the dog all but trains herself— easy and effective. Even when the dog is given run of the house, her first inclination will be to indulge her rewarding chew-toy habit rather than destroy less-attractive household articles, such as curtains, carpets, chairs and compact disks. Similarly, a chew-toy chewer will be less inclined to scratch and chew herself excessively. Also, if the dog busies herself as a recreational chewer, she will be less inclined to develop into a recreational barker or digger when left at home alone.

Stuff a number of chew toys whenever the dog is left confined and remove the extra-special-tasting treats when you return. Your dog will now amuse herself with her chew toys before falling asleep and then resume playing with her chew toys when she expects you to return. Since most owner-absent misbehavior happens right after you leave and right before your expected return, your puppydog will now be conveniently preoccupied with her chew toys at these times.

Come and Sit

Most puppies will happily approach virtually anyone, whether called or not; that is, until they collide with adolescence and

develop other more important doggy interests, such
as sniffing a multiplicity of exquisite odors on the
grass. Your mission, Mr./Ms. Owner, is to teach and
reward the pup for coming reliably, willingly and
happily when called—and you have just three months
to get it done. Unless adequately reinforced, your puppy's tendency to approach people will self-destruct by
adolescence.

Call your dog ("Tina, come!"), open your arms (and
maybe squat down) as a welcoming signal, waggle a
treat or toy as a lure and reward the puppydog when
she comes running. Do not wait to praise the dog until she reaches you—she may come 95 percent of the
way and then run off after some distraction. Instead,
praise the dog's *first* step towards you and continue
praising enthusiastically for *every* step she takes in your
direction.

When the rapidly approaching puppy dog is three
lengths away from impact, instruct her to sit ("Tina,
sit!") and hold the lure in front of you in an outstretched hand to prevent her from hitting you mid-
chest and knocking you flat on your back! As Tina
decelerates to nose the lure, move the treat upwards
and backwards just over her muzzle with an upwards
motion of your extended arm (palm-upwards). As the
dog looks up to follow the lure, she will sit down (if she
jumps up, you are holding the lure too high). Praise
the dog for sitting. Move backwards and call her again.
Repeat this many times over, always praising when Tina
comes and sits; on occasion, reward her.

For the first couple of trials, use a training treat both as
a lure to entice the dog to come and sit and as a reward
for doing so. Thereafter, try to use different items as
lures and rewards. For example, lure the dog with a
Kong or Frisbee but reward her with a food treat. Or
lure the dog with a food treat but pat her and throw a
tennis ball as a reward. After just a few repetitions, dis-
pense with the lures and rewards; the dog will begin to
respond willingly to your verbal requests and hand signals just for the prospect of praise from your heart and
affection from your hands.

Instruct every family member, friend and visitor how to get the dog to come and sit. Invite people over for a series of pooch parties; do not keep the pup a secret— let other people enjoy this puppy, and let the pup enjoy other people. Puppydog parties are not only fun, they easily attract a lot of people to help *you* train *your* dog. Unless you teach your dog how to meet people, that is, to sit for greetings, no doubt the dog will resort to jumping up. Then you and the visitors will get annoyed, and the dog will be punished. This is not fair. *Send out those invitations for puppy parties and teach your dog to be mannerly and socially acceptable.*

Even though your dog quickly masters obedient recalls in the house, her reliability may falter when playing in the backyard or local park. Ironically, it is *the owner* who has unintentionally trained the dog *not* to respond in these instances. By allowing the dog to play and run around and otherwise have a good time, but then to call the dog to put her on leash to take her home, the dog quickly learns playing is fun but training is a drag. Thus, playing in the park becomes a severe distraction, which works against training. Bad news!

Instead, whether playing with the dog off leash or on leash, request her to come at frequent intervals—say, every minute or so. On most occasions, praise and pet the dog for a few seconds while she is sitting, then tell her to go play again. For especially fast recalls, offer a couple of training treats and take the time to praise and pet the dog enthusiastically before releasing her. The dog will learn that coming when called is not necessarily the end of the play session, and neither is it the end of the world; rather, it signals an enjoyable, quality time-out with the owner before resuming play once more. In fact, playing in the park now becomes a very effective life-reward, which works to facilitate training by reinforcing each obedient and timely recall. Good news!

Sit, Down, Stand and Rollover

Teaching the dog a variety of body positions is easy for owner and dog, impressive for spectators and extremely useful for all. Using lure-reward techniques, it is possible to train several positions at once to verbal commands or hand signals (which impress the socks off onlookers).

Sit and ***down***—the two control commands—prevent or resolve nearly a hundred behavior problems. For example, if the dog happily and obediently sits or lies down when requested, she cannot jump on visitors, dash out the front door, run around and chase her tail, pester other dogs, harass cats or annoy family, friends or strangers. Additionally, "Sit" or "Down" are the best emergency commands for off-leash control.

It is easier to teach and maintain a reliable sit than maintain a reliable recall. *Sit* is the purest and simplest of commands—either the dog is sitting or she is not. If there is any change of circumstances or potential danger in the park, for example, simply instruct the dog to sit. If she sits, you have a number of options: Allow the dog to resume playing when she is safe, walk up and put the dog on leash or call the dog. The dog will be much more likely to come when called if she has already acknowledged her compliance by sitting. If the dog does not sit in the park—train her to!

Stand and ***rollover-stay*** are the two positions for examining the dog. Your veterinarian will love you to distraction if you take a little time to teach the dog to stand still and roll over and play possum. Also, your vet bills will be smaller because it will take the veterinarian less time to examine your dog. The rollover-stay is an especially useful command and is really just a variation of the down-stay: Whereas the dog lies prone in the traditional down, she lies supine in the rollover-stay.

As with teaching come and sit, the training techniques to teach the dog to assume all other body positions on cue are user-friendly and dog-friendly. Simply give the appropriate request, lure the dog into the desired body position using a training treat or toy and then *praise* (and maybe reward) the dog as soon as she complies. Try not to touch the dog to get her to respond. If you teach the dog by guiding her into position, the dog will quickly learn that rump-pressure means sit, for example, but as yet you still have no control over your dog if she is just 6 feet away. It will still be necessary to teach the dog to sit on request. So do not make training a time-consuming two-step process; instead, teach the dog to sit to a verbal request or hand signal from the outset. Once the dog sits willingly when requested, by all means use your hands to pet the dog when she does so.

To teach **down** when the dog is already sitting, say "Tina, down!," hold the lure in one hand (palm down) and lower that hand to the floor between the dog's forepaws. As the dog lowers her head to follow the lure, slowly move the lure away from the dog just a fraction (in front of her paws). The dog will lie down as she stretches her nose forward to follow the lure. Praise the dog when she does so. If the dog stands up, you pulled the lure away too far and too quickly.

When teaching the dog to lie down from the standing position, say "Down" and lower the lure to the floor as before. Once the dog has lowered her forequarters and assumed a play bow, gently and slowly move the lure *towards* the dog between her forelegs. Praise the dog as soon as her rear end plops down.

After just a couple of trials it will be possible to alternate sits and downs and have the dog energetically perform doggy push-ups. Praise the dog a lot, and after half a dozen or so push-ups reward the dog with a training treat or toy. You will notice the more energetically you move your arm—upwards (palm up) to get the dog to sit, and downwards (palm down) to get the dog to lie down—the more energetically the dog responds to your requests. Now try training the dog in silence and you will notice she has also learned to respond to hand signals. Yeah! Not too shabby for the first session.

To teach **stand** from the sitting position, say "Tina, stand," slowly move the lure half a dog-length away from the dog's nose, keeping it at nose level, and praise the dog as she stands to follow the lure. As soon

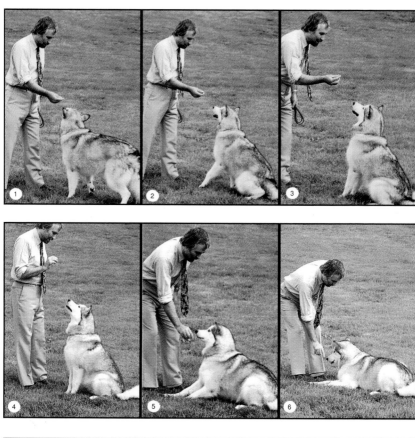

Using a food lure to teach sit, down and stand. 1) "Phoenix, sit." 2) Hand palm upwards, move lure up and back over dog's muzzle. 3) "Good sit, Phoenix!" 4) "Phoenix, down." 5) Hand palm downwards, move lure down to lie between dog's forepaws. 6) "Phoenix, off. Good down, Phoenix!" 7) "Phoenix, sit!" 8) Palm upwards, move lure up and back, keeping it close to dog's muzzle. 9) "Good sit, Phoenix!"

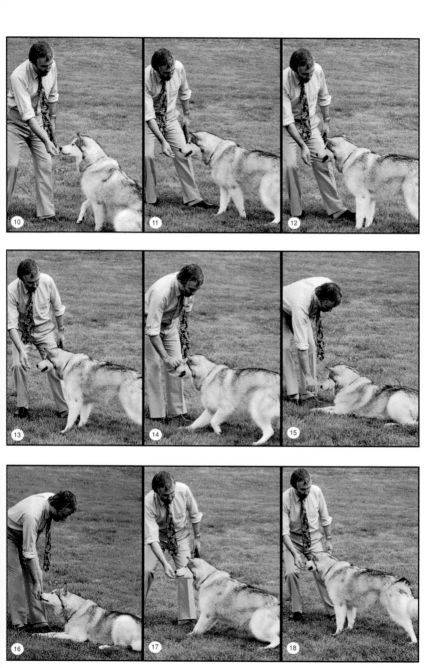

10) *"Phoenix, stand!"* 11) *Move lure away from dog at nose height, then lower it a tad.* 12) *"Phoenix, off! Good stand, Phoenix!"* 13) *"Phoenix, down!"* 14) *Hand palm downwards, move lure down to lie between dog's forepaws.* 15) *"Phoenix, off! Good down-stay, Phoenix!"* 16) *"Phoenix, stand!"* 17) *Move lure away from dog's muzzle up to nose height.* 18) *"Phoenix, off! Good stand-stay, Phoenix. Now we'll make the vet and groomer happy!"*

as the dog stands, lower the lure to just beneath the dog's chin to entice her to look down; otherwise she will stand and then sit immediately. To prompt the dog to stand from the down position, move the lure half a dog-length upwards and away from the dog, holding the lure at standing nose height from the floor.

Teaching *rollover* is best started from the down position, with the dog lying on one side, or at least with both hind legs stretched out on the same side. Say "Tina, bang!" and move the lure backwards and alongside the dog's muzzle to her elbow (on the side of her outstretched hind legs). Once the dog looks to the side and backwards, very slowly move the lure upwards to the dog's shoulder and backbone. Tickling the dog in the goolies (groin area) often invokes a reflex-raising of the hind leg as an appeasement gesture, which facilitates the tendency to roll over. If you move the lure too quickly and the dog jumps into the standing position, have patience and start again. As soon as the dog rolls onto her back, keep the lure stationary and mesmerize the dog with a relaxing tummy rub.

To teach *rollover-stay* when the dog is standing or moving, say "Tina, bang!" and give the appropriate hand signal (with index finger pointed and thumb cocked in true Sam Spade fashion), then in one fluid movement lure her to first lie down and then rollover-stay as above.

Teaching the dog to *stay* in each of the above four positions becomes a piece of cake after first teaching the dog not to worry at the toy or treat training lure. This is best accomplished by hand feeding dinner kibble. Hold a piece of kibble firmly in your hand and softly instruct "Off!" Ignore any licking and slobbering *for however long the dog worries at the treat*, but say "Take it!" and offer the kibble *the instant* the dog breaks contact with her muzzle. Repeat this a few times, and then up the ante and insist the dog remove her muzzle for one whole second before offering the kibble. Then progressively refine your criteria and have the dog not touch your hand (or treat) for longer and longer periods on each trial, such as for two seconds, four seconds, then six, ten, fifteen, twenty, thirty seconds and so on.

The dog soon learns: (1) worrying at the treat never gets results, whereas (2) noncontact is often rewarded after a variable time lapse.

Teaching *"Off!"* has many useful applications in its own right. Additionally, instructing the dog not to touch a training lure often produces spontaneous and magical stays. Request the dog to stand-stay, for example, and not to touch the lure. At first set your sights on a short two-second stay before rewarding the dog. (Remember, every long journey begins with a single step.) However, on subsequent trials, gradually and progressively increase the length of stay required to receive a reward. In no time at all your dog will stand calmly for a minute or so.

Relevancy Training

Once you have taught the dog what you expect her to do when requested to come, sit, lie down, stand, roll-over and stay, the time is right to teach the dog *why* she should comply with your wishes. The secret is to have many (*many*) extremely short training interludes (two to five seconds each) at numerous (*numerous*) times during the course of the dog's day. Especially work with the dog immediately *before* the dog's good times and *during* the dog's good times. For example, ask your dog to sit and/or lie down each time before opening doors, serving meals, offering treats and tummy rubs; ask the dog to perform a few controlled doggy push-ups before letting her off leash or throwing a tennis ball; and perhaps request the dog to sit-down-sit-stand-down-stand-rollover before inviting her to cuddle on the couch.

Similarly, request the dog to sit many times during play or on walks, and in no time at all the dog will be only too pleased to follow your instructions because she has learned that a compliant response heralds all sorts of goodies. Basically all you are trying to teach the dog is how to say please: "Please throw the tennis ball. Please may I snuggle on the couch."

Remember, it is important to keep training interludes short and to have many short sessions each and every day. The shortest (and most useful) session comprises asking the dog to sit and then go play during a play session. When trained this way, your dog will soon associate training with good times. In fact, the dog may be unable to distinguish between training and good times and, indeed, there should be no distinction. The warped concept that training involves forcing the dog to comply and/or dominating her will is totally at odds with the picture of a truly well-trained dog. In reality, enjoying a game of training with a dog is no different from enjoying a game of backgammon or tennis with a friend; and walking with a dog should be no different from strolling with a spouse, or with buddies on the golf course.

Walk by Your Side

Many people attempt to teach a dog to heel by putting her on a leash and physically correcting the dog when she makes mistakes. There are a number of things seriously wrong with this approach, the first being that most people do not want precision heeling; rather, they simply want the dog to follow or walk by their side. Second, when physically restrained during "training," even though the dog may grudgingly mope by your side when "handcuffed" on leash, let's see what happens when she is off leash. History! The dog is in the next county because she never enjoyed walking with you on leash and you have no control over her off leash. So let's just teach the dog off leash from the outset to *want* to walk with us. Third, if the dog has not been trained to heel, it is a trifle hasty to think about punishing the poor dog for making mistakes and breaking heeling rules she didn't even know existed. This is simply not fair! Surely, if the dog had been adequately taught how to heel, she would seldom make mistakes and hence there would be no need to correct the dog. Remember, each mistake and each correction (punishment) advertise the trainer's inadequacy, not the dog's. The dog is not stubborn, she is not stupid and she is not bad. Even if she were, she would still require training, so let's train her properly.

Let's teach the dog to *enjoy* following us and to *want* to walk by our side off leash. Then it will be easier to teach high-precision off-leash heeling patterns if desired. Before going on outdoor walks, it is necessary to teach the dog not to pull. Then it becomes easy to teach on-leash walking and heeling because the dog already wants to walk with you, she is familiar with the desired walking and heeling positions and she knows not to pull.

FOLLOWING

Start by training your dog to follow you. Many puppies will follow if you simply walk away from them and maybe click your fingers or chuckle. Adult dogs may require additional enticement to stimulate them to follow, such as a training lure or, at the very least, a lively trainer. To teach the dog to follow: (1) keep walking and (2) walk away from the dog. If the dog attempts to lead or lag, change pace; slow down if the dog forges too far ahead, but speed up if she lags too far behind. Say "Steady!" or "Easy!" each time before you slow down and "Quickly!" or "Hustle!" each time before you speed up, and the dog will learn to change pace on cue. If the dog lags or leads too far, or if she wanders right or left, simply walk quickly in the opposite direction and maybe even run away from the dog and hide.

Practicing is a lot of fun; you can set up a course in your home, yard or park to do this. Indoors, entice the dog to follow upstairs, into a bedroom, into the bathroom, downstairs, around the living room couch, zigzagging between dining room chairs and into the kitchen for dinner. Outdoors, get the dog to follow around park benches, trees, shrubs and along walkways and lines in the grass. (For safety outdoors, it is advisable to attach a long line on the dog, but never exert corrective tension on the line.)

Remember, following has a lot to do with attitude—*your* attitude! Most probably your dog will *not* want to follow Mr. Grumpy Troll with the personality of wilted lettuce. Lighten up—walk with a jaunty step, whistle a happy tune, sing, skip and tell jokes to your dog and she will be right there by your side.

BY YOUR SIDE

It is smart to train the dog to walk close on one side or the other—either side will do, your choice. When walking, jogging or cycling, it is generally bad news to have the dog suddenly cut in front of you. In fact, I train my dogs to walk "By my side" and "Other side"—both very useful instructions. It is possible to position the dog fairly accurately by looking to the appropriate side and clicking your fingers or slapping your thigh on that side. A precise positioning may be attained by holding a training lure, such as a chew toy, tennis ball or food treat. Stop and stand still several times throughout the walk, just as you would when window shopping or meeting a friend. Use the lure to make sure the dog slows down and stays close whenever you stop.

When teaching the dog to heel, we generally want her to sit in heel position when we stop. Teach heel

Using a toy to teach sit-heel-sit sequences: 1) "Phoenix, sit!" Standing still, move lure up and back over dog's muzzle . . . 2) to position dog sitting in heel position on your left side. 3) Say "Phoenix, heel!" and walk ahead, wagging lure in left hand. Change lure to right hand in preparation for sit signal. Say "Sit" and then . . .

position at the standstill and the dog will learn that the default heel position is sitting by your side (left or right—your choice, unless you wish to compete in obedience trials, in which case the dog must heel on the left).

Several times a day, stand up and call your dog to come and sit in heel position—"Tina, heel!" For example, instruct the dog to come to heel each time there are commercials on TV, or each time you turn a page of a novel, and the dog will get it in a single evening.

Practice straight-line heeling and turns separately. With the dog sitting at heel, teach her to turn in place. After each quarter-turn, half-turn or full turn in place, lure the dog to sit at heel. Now it's time for short straight-line heeling sequences, no more than a few steps at a time. Always think of heeling in terms of sit-heel-sit sequences—start and end with the dog in position and do your best to keep her there when moving. Progressively increase the number of steps in each sequence. When the dog remains close for 20 yards of straight-line heeling, it is time to add a few turns and then sign up for a happy-heeling obedience class to get some advice from the experts.

4) use hand signal to lure dog to sit as you stop. Eventually, dog will sit automatically at heel whenever you stop. 5) "Good dog!"

No Pulling on Leash

You can start teaching your dog not to pull on leash anywhere—in front of the television or outdoors—but regardless of location, you must not take a single step with tension in the leash. For a reason known only to dogs, even just a couple of paces of pulling on leash is intrinsically motivating and diabolically rewarding. Instead, attach the leash to the dog's collar, grasp the other end firmly with both hands held close to your chest, and stand still—do not budge an inch. Have somebody watch you with a stopwatch to time your progress, or else you will never believe this will work and so you will not even try the exercise, and your shoulder and the dog's neck will be traumatized for years to come.

Stand still and wait for the dog to stop pulling, and to sit and/or lie down. All dogs stop pulling and sit eventually. Most take only a couple of minutes; the all-time record is 22½ minutes. Time how long it takes. Gently praise the dog when she stops pulling, and as soon as she sits, enthusiastically praise the dog and take just one step forward, then immediately stand still. This single step usually demonstrates the ballistic reinforcing nature of pulling on leash; most dogs explode to the end of the leash, so be prepared for the strain. Stand firm and wait for the dog to sit again. Repeat this half a dozen times and you will probably notice a progressive reduction in the force of the dog's one-step explosions and a radical reduction in the time it takes for the dog to sit each time.

As the dog learns "Sit we go" and "Pull we stop," she will begin to walk forward calmly with each single step and automatically sit when you stop. Now try two steps before you stop. Wooooooo! Scary! When the dog has mastered two steps at a time, try for three. After each success, progressively increase the number of steps in the sequence: try four steps and then six, eight, ten and twenty steps before stopping. Congratulations! You are now walking the dog on leash.

Whenever walking with the dog (off leash or on leash), make sure you stop periodically to practice a few position commands and stays before instructing the dog to "Walk on!" (Remember, you want the dog to be compliant everywhere, not just in the kitchen when her dinner is at hand.) For example, stopping every 25 yards to briefly train the dog amounts to over 200 training interludes within a single 3-mile stroll. And each training session is in a different location. You will not believe the improvement within just the first mile of the first walk.

To put it another way, integrating training into a walk offers 200 separate opportunities to use the continuance of the walk as a reward to reinforce the dog's education. Moreover, some training interludes may comprise continuing education for the dog's walking skills: Alternate short periods of the dog walking calmly by your side with periods when the dog is allowed to sniff and investigate the environment. Now sniffing odors on the grass and meeting other dogs become rewards which reinforce the dog's calm and mannerly demeanor. Good Lord! Whatever next? Many enjoyable walks together of course. Happy trails!

THE IMPORTANCE OF TRICKS

Nothing will improve a dog's quality of life better than having a few tricks under her belt. Teaching any trick expands the dog's vocabulary, which facilitates communication and improves the owner's control. Also, specific tricks help prevent and resolve specific behavior problems. For example, by teaching the dog to fetch her toys, the dog learns carrying a toy makes the owner happy and, therefore, will be more likely to chew her toy than other inappropriate items.

More important, teaching tricks prompts owners to lighten up and train with a sunny disposition. Really, tricks should be no different from any other behaviors we put on cue. But they are. When teaching tricks, owners have a much sweeter attitude, which in turn motivates the dog and improves her willingness to comply. The dog feels tricks are a blast, but formal commands are a drag. In fact, tricks are so enjoyable, they may be used as rewards in training by asking the dog to come, sit and down-stay and then rollover for a tummy rub. Go on, try it: Crack a smile and even giggle when the dog promptly and willingly lies down and stays.

Most important, performing tricks prompts onlookers to smile and giggle. Many people are scared of dogs, especially large ones. And nothing can be more off-putting for a dog than to be constantly confronted by strangers who don't like her because of her size or the way she looks. Uneasy people put the dog on edge, causing her to back off and bark, only frightening people all the more. And so a vicious circle develops, with the people's fear fueling the dog's fear *and vice versa.* Instead, tie a pink ribbon to your dog's collar and practice all sorts of tricks on walks and in the park, and you will be pleasantly amazed how it changes people's attitudes toward your friendly dog. The dog's repertoire of tricks is limited only by the trainer's imagination. Below I have described three of my favorites:

SPEAK AND SHUSH

The training sequence involved in teaching a dog to bark on request is no different from that used when training any behavior on cue: request—lure—response—reward. As always, the secret of success lies in finding an effective lure. If the dog always barks at the doorbell, for example, say "Rover, speak!", have an accomplice ring the doorbell, then reward the dog for barking. After a few woofs, ask Rover to "Shush!", waggle a food treat under her nose (to entice her to sniff and thus to shush), praise her when quiet and eventually offer the treat as a reward. Alternate "Speak" and "Shush," progressively increasing the length of shush-time between each barking bout.

PLAY BOW

With the dog standing, say "Bow!" and lower the food lure (palm upwards) to rest between the dog's forepaws. Praise as the dog lowers

her forequarters and sternum to the ground (as when teaching the down), but then lure the dog to stand and offer the treat. On successive trials, gradually increase the length of time the dog is required to remain in the play bow posture in order to gain a food reward. If the dog's rear end collapses into a down, say nothing and offer no reward; simply start over.

BE A BEAR

With the dog sitting backed into a corner to prevent her from toppling over backwards, say "Be a bear!" With bent paw and palm down, raise a lure upwards and backwards along the top of the dog's muzzle. Praise the dog when she sits up on her haunches and offer the treat as a reward. To prevent the dog from standing on her hind legs, keep the lure closer to the dog's muzzle. On each trial, progressively increase the length of time the dog is required to sit up to receive a food reward. Since lure-reward training is so easy, teach the dog to stand and walk on her hind legs as well!

Teaching "Be a Bear"

chapter 9

Getting

Active

with your Dog

by Bardi McLennan

Once you and your dog have graduated from basic obedience training and are beginning to work together as a team, you can take part in the growing world of dog activities. There are so many fun things to do with your dog! Just remember, people and dogs don't always learn at the same pace, so don't be upset if you (or your dog) need more than two basic training courses before your team becomes operational. Even smart dogs don't go straight to college from kindergarten!

Just as there are events geared to certain types of dogs, so there are ones that are more appealing to certain types of people. In some activities, you give the commands and your dog does the work (upland game hunting is one example), while in others, such as agility, you'll both get a workout. You may want to aim for prestigious titles to add to your dog's name, or you may want nothing more than the sheer enjoyment of being around other people and their dogs. Passive or active, participation has its own rewards.

Consider your dog's physical capabilities when looking into any of the canine activities. It's easy to see that a Basset Hound is not built for the racetrack, nor would a Chihuahua be the breed of choice for pulling a sled. A loyal dog will attempt almost anything you ask him to do, so it is up to you to know your dog's limitations. A dog must be physically sound in order to compete at any level in athletic activities, and being mentally sound is a definite plus. Advanced age, however, may not be a deterrent. Many dogs still hunt and herd at ten or twelve years of age. It's entirely possible for dogs to be "fit at 50." Take your dog for a checkup, explain to your vet the type of activity you have in mind and be guided by his or her findings.

All dogs seem to love playing flyball.

You needn't be restricted to breed-specific sports if it's only fun you're after. Certain AKC activities are limited to designated breeds; however, as each new trial, test or sport has grown in popularity, so has the variety of breeds encouraged to participate at a fun level.

But don't shortchange your fun, or that of your dog, by thinking only of the basic function of her breed. Once a dog has learned how to learn, she can be taught to do just about anything as long as the size of the dog is right for the job and you both think it is fun and rewarding. In other words, you are a team.

To get involved in any of the activities detailed in this chapter, look for the names and addresses of the organizations that sponsor them in Chapter 13. You can also ask your breeder or a local dog trainer for contacts.

You can compete in obedience trials with a well trained dog.

Official American Kennel Club Activities

The following tests and trials are some of the events sanctioned by the AKC and sponsored by various dog clubs. Your dog's expertise will be rewarded with impressive titles. You can participate just for fun, or be competitive and go for those awards.

OBEDIENCE

Training classes begin with pups as young as three months of age in kindergarten puppy training, then advance to pre-novice (all exercises on lead) and go on to novice, which is where you'll start off-lead work. In obedience classes dogs learn to sit, stay, heel and come through a variety of exercises. Once you've got the basics down, you can enter obedience trials and work toward earning your dog's first degree, a C.D. (Companion Dog).

The next level is called "Open," in which jumps and retrieves perk up the dog's interest. Passing grades in competition at this level earn a C.D.X. (Companion Dog Excellent). Beyond that lies the goal of the most ambitious—Utility (U.D. and even U.D.X. or OTCh, an Obedience Champion).

AGILITY

All dogs can participate in the latest canine sport to have gained worldwide popularity for its fun and excitement, agility. It began in England as a canine version of horse show-jumping, but because dogs are more agile and able to perform on verbal commands, extra feats were added such as climbing, balancing and racing through tunnels or in and out of weave poles. Many of the obstacles (regulation or homemade) can be set up in your own backyard. If the agility bug bites, you could end up in international competition!

For starters, your dog should be obedience trained, even though, in the beginning, the lessons may all be taught on lead. Once the dog understands the commands (and you do, too), it's as easy as guiding the dog over a prescribed course, one obstacle at a time. In competition, the race is against the clock, so wear your running shoes! The dog starts with 200 points and the judge deducts for infractions and misadventures along the way.

All dogs seem to love agility and respond to it as if they were being turned loose in a playground paradise. Your dog's enthusiasm will be contagious; agility turns into great fun for dog and owner.

FIELD TRIALS AND HUNTING TESTS

There are field trials and hunting tests for the sporting breeds—retrievers, spaniels and pointing breeds, and for some hounds—Bassets, Beagles and Dachshunds. Field trials are competitive events that test a dog's ability to perform the functions for which she was bred. Hunting tests, which are open to retrievers,

---

TITLES AWARDED BY THE AKC

Conformation: Ch. (Champion)

Obedience: CD (Companion Dog); CDX (Companion Dog Excellent); UD (Utility Dog); UDX (Utility Dog Excellent); OTCh. (Obedience Trial Champion)

Field: JH (Junior Hunter); SH (Senior Hunter); MH (Master Hunter); AFCh. (Amateur Field Champion); FCh. (Field Champion)

Lure Coursing: JC (Junior Courser); SC (Senior Courser)

Herding: HT (Herding Tested); PT (Pre-Trial Tested); HS (Herding Started); HI (Herding Intermediate); HX (Herding Excellent); HCh. (Herding Champion)

Tracking: TD (Tracking Dog); TDX (Tracking Dog Excellent)

Agility: NAD (Novice Agility); OAD (Open Agility); ADX (Agility Excellent); MAX (Master Agility)

Earthdog Tests: JE (Junior Earthdog); SE (Senior Earthdog); ME (Master Earthdog)

Canine Good Citizen: CGC

Combination: DC (Dual Champion—Ch. and Fch.); TC (Triple Champion—Ch., Fch., and OTCh.)

spaniels and pointing breeds only, are noncompetitive and are a means of judging the dog's ability as well as that of the handler.

Hunting is a very large and complex part of canine sports, and if you own one of the breeds that hunts, the events are a great treat for your dog and you. He gets to do what he was bred for, and you get to work with him and watch him do it. You'll be proud of and amazed at what your dog can do.

Fortunately, the AKC publishes a series of booklets on these events, which outline the rules and regulations and include a glossary of the sometimes complicated terms. The AKC also publishes newsletters for field trialers and hunting test enthusiasts. The United Kennel Club (UKC) also has informative materials for the hunter and his dog.

Retrievers and other sporting breeds get to do what they're bred to in hunting tests.

HERDING TESTS AND TRIALS

Herding, like hunting, dates back to the first known uses man made of dogs. The interest in herding today is widespread, and if you own a herding breed, you can join in the activity. Herding dogs are tested for their natural skills to keep a flock of ducks, sheep or cattle together. If your dog shows potential, you can start at the testing level, where your dog can earn a title for showing an inherent herding ability. With training you can advance to the trial level, where your dog should be capable of controlling even difficult livestock in diverse situations.

LURE COURSING

The AKC Tests and Trials for Lure Coursing are open to traditional sighthounds—Greyhounds, Whippets,

Borzoi, Salukis, Afghan Hounds, Ibizan Hounds and Scottish Deerhounds—as well as to Basenjis and Rhodesian Ridgebacks. Hounds are judged on overall ability, follow, speed, agility and endurance. This is possibly the most exciting of the trials for spectators, because the speed and agility of the dogs is awesome to watch as they chase the lure (or "course") in heats of two or three dogs at a time.

Tracking

Tracking is another activity in which almost any dog can compete because every dog that sniffs the ground when taken outdoors is, in fact, tracking. The hard part comes when the rules as to what, when and where the dog tracks are determined by a person, not the dog! Tracking tests cover a large area of fields, woods and roads. The tracks are laid hours before the dogs go to work on them, and include "tricks" like cross-tracks and sharp turns. If you're interested in search-and-rescue work, this is the place to start.

This tracking dog is hot on the trail.

Earthdog Tests for Small Terriers and Dachshunds

These tests are open to Australian, Bedlington, Border, Cairn, Dandie Dinmont, Smooth and Wire Fox, Lakeland, Norfolk, Norwich, Scottish, Sealyham, Skye, Welsh and West Highland White Terriers as well as Dachshunds. The dogs need no prior training for this terrier sport. There is a qualifying test on the day of the event, so dog and handler learn the rules on the spot. These tests, or "digs," sometimes end with informal races in the late afternoon.

133

Here are some of the extracurricular obedience and racing activities that are not regulated by the AKC or UKC, but are generally run by clubs or a group of dog fanciers and are often open to all.

Canine Freestyle This activity is something new on the scene and is variously likened to dancing, dressage or ice skating. It is meant to show the athleticism of the dog, but also requires showmanship on the part of the dog's handler. If you and your dog like to ham it up for friends, you might want to look into freestyle.

Lure coursing lets sighthounds do what they do best—run!

Scent Hurdle Racing Scent hurdle racing is purely a fun activity sponsored by obedience clubs with members forming competing teams. The height of the hurdles is based on the size of the shortest dog on the team. On a signal, one team dog is released on each of two side-by-side courses and must clear every hurdle before picking up its own dumbbell from a platform and returning over the jumps to the handler. As each dog returns, the next on that team is sent. Of course, that is what the dogs are supposed to do. When the dogs improvise (going under or around the hurdles, stealing another dog's dumbbell, and so forth), it no doubt frustrates the handlers, but just adds to the fun for everyone else.

Flyball This type of racing is similar, but after negotiating the four hurdles, the dog comes to a flyball box, steps on a lever that releases a tennis ball into the air, catches the ball and returns over the hurdles to the starting point. This game also becomes extremely fun for spectators because the dogs sometimes cheat by catching a ball released by the dog in the next lane. Three titles can be earned—Flyball Dog (F.D.), Flyball Dog Excellent (F.D.X.) and Flyball Dog Champion (Fb.D.Ch.)—all awarded by the North American Flyball Association, Inc.

Dogsledding The name conjures up the Rocky Mountains or the frigid North, but you can find dogsled clubs in such unlikely spots as Maryland, North Carolina and Virginia! Dogsledding is primarily for the Nordic breeds such as the Alaskan Malamutes, Siberian Huskies and Samoyeds, but other breeds can try. There are some practical backyard applications to this sport, too. With parental supervision, almost any strong dog could pull a child's sled.

Coming over the A-frame on an agility course.

These are just some of the many recreational ways you can get to know and understand your multifaceted dog better and have fun doing it.

chapter 10

Your Dog
and your
Family

by Bardi McLennan

Adding a dog automatically increases your family by one, no matter whether you live alone in an apartment or are part of a mother, father and six kids household. The single-person family is fair game for numerous and varied canine misconceptions as to who is dog and who pays the bills, whereas a dog in a houseful of children will consider himself to be just one of the gang, littermates all. One dog and one child may give a dog reason to believe they are both kids or both dogs.

Either interpretation requires parental supervision and sometimes speedy intervention.

As soon as one paw goes through the door into your home, Rufus (or Rufina) has to make many adjustments to become a part of your

136

family. Your job is to make him fit in as painlessly as possible. An older dog may have some frame of reference from past experience, but to a 10-week-old puppy, everything is brand new: people, furniture, stairs, when and where people eat, sleep or watch TV, his own place and everyone else's space, smells, sounds, outdoors—everything!

Puppies, and newly acquired dogs of any age, do not need what we think of as "freedom." If you leave a new dog or puppy loose in the house, you will almost certainly return to chaotic destruction and the dog will forever after equate your homecoming with a time of punishment to be dreaded. It is unfair to give your dog what amounts to "freedom to get into trouble." Instead, confine him to a crate for brief periods of your absence (up to three or four hours) and, for the long haul, a workday for example, confine him to one untrashable area with his own toys, a bowl of water and a radio left on (low) in another room.

Lots of pets get along with each other just fine.

For the first few days, when not confined, put Rufus on a long leash tied to your wrist or waist. This umbilical cord method enables the dog to learn all about you from your body language and voice, and to learn by his own actions which things in the house are NO! and which ones are rewarded by "Good dog." House-training will be easier with the pup always by your side. Speaking of which, accidents do happen. That goal of "completely housetrained" takes up to a year, or the length of time it takes the pup to mature.

The All-Adult Family

Most dogs in an adults-only household today are likely to be latchkey pets, with no one home all day but the dog. When you return after a tough day on the job, the dog can and should be your relaxation therapy. But going home can instead be a daily frustration.

Separation anxiety is a very common problem for the dog in a working household. It may begin with whines and barks of loneliness, but it will soon escalate into a frenzied destruction derby. That is why it is so important to set aside the time to teach a dog to relax when left alone in his confined area and to understand that he can trust you to return.

Let the dog get used to your work schedule in easy stages. Confine him to one room and go in and out of that room over and over again. Be casual about it. No physical, voice or eye contact. When the pup no longer even notices your comings and goings, leave the house for varying lengths of time, returning to stay home for a few minutes and gradually increasing the time away. This training can take days, but the dog is learning that you haven't left him forever and that he can trust you.

Any time you leave the dog, but especially during this training period, be casual about your departure. No anxiety-building fond farewells. Just "Bye" and go! Remember the "Good dog" when you return to find everything more or less as you left it.

If things are a mess (or even a disaster) when you return, greet the dog, take him outside to eliminate, and then put him in his crate while you clean up. Rant and rave in the shower! *Do not* punish the dog. You were not there when it happened, and the rule is: Only punish as you catch the dog in the act of wrongdoing. Obviously, it makes sense to get your latchkey puppy when you'll have a week or two to spend on these training essentials.

Family weekend activities should include Rufus whenever possible. Depending on the pup's age, now is the time for a long walk in the park, playtime in the backyard, a hike in the woods. Socializing is as important as health care, good food and physical exercise, so visiting Aunt Emma or Uncle Harry and the next-door neighbor's dog or cat is essential to developing an out-going, friendly temperament in your pet.

If you are a single adult, socializing Rufus at home and away will prevent him from becoming overly protective of you (or just overly attached) and will also prevent such behavioral problems as dominance or fear of strangers.

Babies

Whether already here or on the way, babies figure larger than life in the eyes of a dog. If the dog is there first, let him in on all your baby preparations in the house. When baby arrives, let Rufus sniff any item of clothing that has been on the baby before Junior comes home. Then let Mom greet the dog first before introducing the new family member. Hold the baby down for the dog to see and sniff, but make sure some-

one's holding the dog on lead in case of any sudden moves. Don't play keep-away or tease the dog with the baby, which only invites undesirable jumping up.

The dog and the baby are "family," and for starters can be treated almost as equals. Things rapidly change, however, especially when baby takes to creeping around on all fours on the dog's turf or, better yet, has yummy pudding all over her face and hands! That's when a lot of things in the dog's and baby's lives become more separate than equal.

Dogs are perfect confidants.

Toddlers make terrible dog owners, but if you can't avoid the combination, use patient discipline (that is, positive teaching rather than punishment), and use time-outs before you run out of patience.

139

A dog and a baby (or toddler, or an assertive young child) should never be left alone together. Take the dog with you or confine him. With a baby or youngsters in the house, you'll have plenty of use for that wonderful canine safety device called a crate!

Young Children

Any dog in a house with kids will behave pretty much as the kids do, good or bad. But even good dogs and good children can get into trouble when play becomes rowdy and active.

Teach children how to play nicely with a puppy.

Legs bobbing up and down, shrill voices screeching, a ball hurtling overhead, all add up to exuberant frustration for a dog who's just trying to be part of the gang. In a pack of puppies, any legs or toys being chased would be caught by a set of teeth, and all the pups involved would understand that is how the game is played. Kids do not understand this, nor do parents tolerate it. Bring Rufus indoors before you have reason to regret it. This is time-out, not a punishment.

You can explain the situation to the children and tell them they must play quieter games until the puppy learns not to grab them with his mouth. Unfortunately, you can't explain it that easily to the dog. With adult supervision, they will learn how to play together.

Young children love to tease. Sticking their faces or wiggling their hands or fingers in the dog's face is teasing. To another person it might be just annoying, but it is threatening to a dog. There's another difference: We can make the child stop by an explanation, but the only way a dog can stop it is with a warning growl and then with teeth. Teasing is the major cause of children being bitten by their pets. Treat it seriously.

140

Older Children

The best age for a child to get a first dog is between the ages of 8 and 12. That's when kids are able to accept some real responsibility for their pet. Even so, take the child's vow of "I will never *ever* forget to feed (brush, walk, etc.) the dog" for what it's worth: a child's good intention at that moment. Most kids today have extra lessons, soccer practice, Little League, ballet, and so forth piled on top of school schedules. There will be many times when Mom will have to come to the dog's rescue. "I walked the dog for you so you can set the table for me" is one way to get around a missed appointment without laying on blame or guilt.

Kids in this age group make excellent obedience trainers because they are into the teaching/learning process themselves and they lack the self-consciousness of adults. Attending a dog show is something the whole family can enjoy, and watching Junior Showmanship may catch the eye of the kids. Older children can begin to get involved in many of the recreational activities that were reviewed in the previous chapter. Some of the agility obstacles, for example, can be set up in the backyard as a family project (with an adult making sure all the equipment is safe and secure for the dog).

Older kids are also beginning to look to the future, and may envision themselves as veterinarians or trainers or show dog handlers or writers of the next Lassie best-seller. Dogs are perfect confidants for these dreams. They won't tell a soul.

Other Pets

Introduce all pets tactfully. In a dog/cat situation, hold the dog, not the cat. Let two dogs meet on neutral turf—a stroll in the park or a walk down the street—with both on loose leads to permit all the normal canine ways of saying hello, including routine sniffing, circling, more sniffing, and so on. Small creatures such as hamsters, chinchillas or mice must be kept safe from their natural predators (dogs and cats).

141

Festive Family Occasions

Parties are great for people, but not necessarily for puppies. Until all the guests have arrived, put the dog in his crate or in a room where he won't be disturbed. A socialized dog can join the fun later as long as he's not underfoot, annoying guests or into the hors d'oeuvres.

There are a few dangers to consider, too. Doors opening and closing can allow a puppy to slip out unnoticed in the confusion, and you'll be organizing a search party instead of playing host or hostess. Party food and buffet service are not for dogs. Let Rufus party in his crate with a nice big dog biscuit.

At Christmas time, not only are tree decorations dangerous and breakable (and perhaps family heirlooms), but extreme caution should be taken with the lights, cords and outlets for the tree lights and any other festive lighting. Occasionally a dog lifts a leg, ignoring the fact that the tree is indoors. To avoid this, use a canine repellent, made for gardens, on the tree. Or keep him out of the tree room unless supervised. And whatever you do, *don't* invite trouble by hanging his toys on the tree!

Car Travel

Before you plan a vacation by car or RV with Rufus, be sure he enjoys car travel. Nothing spoils a holiday quicker than a carsick dog! Work within the dog's comfort level. Get in the car with the dog in his crate or attached to a canine car safety belt and just sit there until he relaxes. That's all. Next time, get in the car, turn on the engine and go nowhere. Just sit. When that is okay, turn on the engine and go around the block. Now you can go for a ride and include a stop where you get out, leaving the dog for a minute or two.

On a warm day, always park in the shade and leave windows open several inches. And return quickly. It only takes 10 minutes for a car to become an overheated steel death trap.

Motel or Pet Motel?

Not all motels or hotels accept pets, but you have a much better choice today than even a few years ago. To find a dog-friendly lodging, look at *On the Road Again With Man's Best Friend*, a series of directories that detail bed and breakfasts, inns, family resorts and other hotels/motels. Some places require a refundable deposit to cover any damage incurred by the dog. More B&Bs accept pets now, but some restrict the size.

If taking Rufus with you is not feasible, check out boarding kennels in your area. Your veterinarian may offer this service, or recommend a kennel or two he or she is familiar with. Go see the facilities for yourself, ask about exercise, diet, housing, and so on. Or, if you'd rather have Rufus stay home, look into bonded petsitters, many of whom will also bring in the mail and water your plants.

chapter 11

Your Dog
and your
Community

by Bardi McLennan

Step outside your home with your dog and you are no longer just family, you are both part of your community. This is when the phrase "responsible pet ownership" takes on serious implications. For starters, it means you pick up after your dog—not just occasionally, but every time your dog eliminates away from home. That means you have joined the Plastic Baggy Brigade! You always have plastic sandwich bags in your pocket and several in the car. It means you teach your kids how to use them, too. If you think this is "yucky," just imagine what the person (a non-doggy person) who inadvertently steps in the mess thinks!

Your responsibility extends to your neighbors: To their ears (no annoying barking); to their property (their garbage, their lawn, their flower beds, their cat—especially their cat); to their kids (on bikes, at play); to their kids' toys and sports equipment.

There are numerous dog-related laws, ranging from simple dog licensing and leash laws to those holding you liable for any physical injury or property damage done by your dog. These laws are in place to protect everyone in the community, including you and your dog. There are town ordinances and state laws which are by no means the same in all towns or all states. Ignorance of the law won't get you off the hook. The time to find out what the laws are where you live is now.

Be sure your dog's license is current. This is not just a good local ordinance, it can make the difference between finding your lost dog or not.

Dressing your dog up makes him appealing to strangers.

Many states now require proof of rabies vaccination and that the dog has been spayed or neutered before issuing a license. At the same time, keep up the dog's annual immunizations.

Never let your dog run loose in the neighborhood. This will not only keep you on the right side of the leash law, it's the outdoor version of the rule about not giving your dog "freedom to get into trouble."

Good Canine Citizen

Sometimes it's hard for a dog's owner to assess whether or not the dog is sufficiently socialized to be accepted by the community at large. Does Rufus or Rufina display good, controlled behavior in public? The AKC's Canine Good Citizen program is available through many dog organizations. If your dog passes the test, the title "CGC" is earned.

The overall purpose is to turn your dog into a good neighbor and to teach you about your responsibility to your community as a dog owner. Here are the ten things your dog must do willingly:

1. Accept a stranger stopping to chat with you.
2. Sit and be petted by a stranger.
3. Allow a stranger to handle him or her as a groomer or veterinarian would.
4. Walk nicely on a loose lead.
5. Walk calmly through a crowd.
6. Sit and down on command, then stay in a sit or down position while you walk away.
7. Come when called.
8. Casually greet another dog.
9. React confidently to distractions.
10. Accept being left alone with someone other than you and not become overly agitated or nervous.

Schools and Dogs

Schools are getting involved with pet ownership on an educational level. It has been proven that children who are kind to animals are humane in their attitude toward other people as adults.

A dog is a child's best friend, and so children are often primary pet owners, if not the primary caregivers. Unfortunately, they are also the ones most often bitten by dogs. This occurs due to a lack of understanding that pets, no matter how sweet, cuddly and loving, are still animals. Schools, along with parents, dog clubs, dog fanciers and the AKC, are working to change all that with video programs for children not only in grade school, but in the nursery school and pre-kindergarten age group. Teaching youngsters how to be responsible dog owners is important community work. When your dog has a CGC, volunteer to take part in an educational classroom event put on by your dog club.

Boy Scout Merit Badge

A Merit Badge for Dog Care can be earned by any Boy Scout ages 11 to 18. The requirements are not easy, but amount to a complete course in responsible dog care and general ownership. Here are just a few of the things a Scout must do to earn that badge:

Point out ten parts of the dog using the correct names.

Give a report (signed by parent or guardian) on your care of the dog (feeding, food used, housing, exercising, grooming and bathing), plus what has been done to keep the dog healthy.

Explain the right way to obedience train a dog, and demonstrate three comments.

Several of the requirements have to do with health care, including first aid, handling a hurt dog, and the dangers of home treatment for a serious ailment.

The final requirement is to know the local laws and ordinances involving dogs.

There are similar programs for Girl Scouts and 4-H members.

Local Clubs

Local dog clubs are no longer in existence just to put on a yearly dog show. Today, they are apt to be the hub of the community's involvement with pets. Dog clubs conduct educational forums with big-name speakers, stage demonstrations of canine talent in a busy mall and take dogs of various breeds to schools for class-room discussion.

The quickest way to feel accepted as a member in a club is to volunteer your services! Offer to help with something—anything—and watch your popularity (and your interest) grow.

Therapy Dogs

Once your dog has earned that essential CGC and reliably demonstrates a steady, calm temperament, you could look into what therapy dogs are doing in your area.

Therapy dogs go with their owners to visit patients at hospitals or nursing homes, generally remaining on leash but able to coax a pat from a stiffened hand, a smile from a blank face, a few words from sealed lips or a hug from someone in need of love.

Nursing homes cover a wide range of patient care. Some specialize in care of the elderly, some in the treatment of specific illnesses, some in physical therapy. Children's facilities also welcome visits from trained therapy dogs for boosting morale in their pediatric patients. Hospice care for the terminally ill and the at-home care of AIDS patients are other areas where this canine visiting is desperately needed. Therapy dog training comes first.

Your dog can make a difference in lots of lives.

There is a lot more involved than just taking your nice friendly pooch to someone's bedside. Doing therapy dog work involves your own emotional stability as well as that of your dog. But once you have met all the requirements for this work, making the rounds once a week or once a month with your therapy dog is possibly the most rewarding of all community activities.

Disaster Aid

This community service is definitely not for everyone, partly because it is time-consuming. The initial training is rigorous, and there can be no let-up in the continuing workouts, because members are on call 24 hours a day to go wherever they are needed at a moment's notice. But if you think you would like to be able to assist in a disaster, look into search-and-rescue work. The network of search-and-rescue volunteers is worldwide, and all members of the American Rescue Dog Association (ARDA) who are qualified to do this work are volunteers who train and maintain their own dogs.

Physical Aid

Most people are familiar with Seeing Eye dogs, which serve as blind people's eyes, but not with all the other work that dogs are trained to do to assist the disabled. Dogs are also specially trained to pull wheelchairs, carry school books, pick up dropped objects, open and close doors. Some also are ears for the deaf. All these assistance-trained dogs, by the way, are allowed anywhere "No Pet" signs exist (as are therapy dogs when

Making the rounds with your therapy dog can be very rewarding.

properly identified). Getting started in any of this fascinating work requires a background in dog training and canine behavior, but there are also volunteer jobs ranging from answering the phone to cleaning out kennels to providing a foster home for a puppy. You have only to ask.

part four

Beyond
the
Basics

Recommended Reading

Books

ABOUT HEALTH CARE

Ackerman, Lowell. *Guide to Skin and Haircoat Problems in Dogs.* Loveland, Colo.: Alpine Publications, 1994.

Alderton, David. *The Dog Care Manual.* Hauppauge, N.Y.: Barron's Educational Series, Inc., 1986.

American Kennel Club. *American Kennel Club Dog Care and Training.* New York: Howell Book House, 1991.

Bamberger, Michelle, DVM. *Help! The Quick Guide to First Aid for Your Dog.* New York: Howell Book House, 1995.

Carlson, Delbert, DVM, and James Giffin, MD. *Dog Owner's Home Veterinary Handbook.* New York: Howell Book House, 1992.

DeBitetto, James, DVM, and Sarah Hodgson. *You & Your Puppy.* New York: Howell Book House, 1995.

Humphries, Jim, DVM. *Dr. Jim's Animal Clinic for Dogs.* New York: Howell Book House, 1994.

McGinnis, Terri. *The Well Dog Book.* New York: Random House, 1991.

Pitcairn, Richard and Susan. *Natural Health for Dogs.* Emmaus, Pa.: Rodale Press, 1982.

ABOUT DOG SHOWS

Hall, Lynn. *Dog Showing for Beginners.* New York: Howell Book House, 1994.

Nichols, Virginia Tuck. *How to Show Your Own Dog.* Neptune, N. J.: TFH, 1970.

Vanacore, Connie. *Dog Showing, An Owner's Guide.* New York: Howell Book House, 1990.

ABOUT TRAINING

Ammen, Amy. *Training in No Time*. New York: Howell Book House, 1995.

Baer, Ted. *Communicating With Your Dog*. Hauppauge, N.Y.: Barron's Educational Series, Inc., 1989.

Benjamin, Carol Lea. *Dog Problems*. New York: Howell Book House, 1989.

Benjamin, Carol Lea. *Dog Training for Kids*. New York: Howell Book House, 1988.

Benjamin, Carol Lea. *Mother Knows Best*. New York: Howell Book House, 1985.

Benjamin, Carol Lea. *Surviving Your Dog's Adolescence*. New York: Howell Book House, 1993.

Bohnenkamp, Gwen. *Manners for the Modern Dog*. San Francisco: Perfect Paws, 1990.

Dibra, Bashkim. *Dog Training by Bash*. New York: Dell, 1992.

Dunbar, Ian, PhD, MRCVS. *Dr. Dunbar's Good Little Dog Book*, James & Kenneth Publishers, 2140 Shattuck Ave. #2406, Berkeley, Calif. 94704. (510) 658–8588. Order from the publisher.

Dunbar, Ian, PhD, MRCVS. *How to Teach a New Dog Old Tricks*, James & Kenneth Publishers. Order from the publisher; address above.

Dunbar, Ian, PhD, MRCVS, and Gwen Bohnenkamp. Booklets on *Preventing Aggression; Housetraining; Chewing; Digging; Barking; Socialization; Fearfulness; and Fighting*, James & Kenneth Publishers. Order from the publisher; address above.

Evans, Job Michael. *People, Pooches and Problems*. New York: Howell Book House, 1991.

Kilcommons, Brian and Sarah Wilson. *Good Owners, Great Dogs*. New York: Warner Books, 1992.

McMains, Joel M. *Dog Logic—Companion Obedience*. New York: Howell Book House, 1992.

Rutherford, Clarice and David H. Neil, MRCVS. *How to Raise a Puppy You Can Live With*. Loveland, Colo.: Alpine Publications, 1982.

Volhard, Jack and Melissa Bartlett. *What All Good Dogs Should Know: The Sensible Way to Train*. New York: Howell Book House, 1991.

ABOUT BREEDING

Harris, Beth J. Finder. *Breeding a Litter, The Complete Book of Prenatal and Postnatal Care*. New York: Howell Book House, 1983.

Holst, Phyllis, DVM. *Canine Reproduction*. Loveland, Colo.: Alpine Publications, 1985.

Walkowicz, Chris and Bonnie Wilcox, DVM. *Successful Dog Breeding, The Complete Handbook of Canine Midwifery*. New York: Howell Book House, 1994.

ABOUT ACTIVITIES

American Rescue Dog Association. *Search and Rescue Dogs*. New York: Howell Book House, 1991.

Barwig, Susan and Stewart Hilliard. *Schutzhund*. New York: Howell Book House, 1991.

Beaman, Arthur S. *Lure Coursing*. New York: Howell Book House, 1994.

Daniels, Julie. *Enjoying Dog Agility—From Backyard to Competition*. New York: Doral Publishing, 1990.

Davis, Kathy Diamond. *Therapy Dogs*. New York: Howell Book House, 1992.

Gallup, Davis Anne. *Running With Man's Best Friend*. Loveland, Colo.: Alpine Publications, 1986.

Habgood, Dawn and Robert. *On the Road Again With Man's Best Friend*. New England, Mid-Atlantic, West Coast and Southeast editions. Selective guides to area bed and breakfasts, inns, hotels and resorts that welcome guests and their dogs. New York: Howell Book House, 1995.

Holland, Vergil S. *Herding Dogs*. New York: Howell Book House, 1994.

LaBelle, Charlene G. *Backpacking With Your Dog*. Loveland, Colo.: Alpine Publications, 1993.

Simmons-Moake, Jane. *Agility Training, The Fun Sport for All Dogs*. New York: Howell Book House, 1991.

Spencer, James B. *Hup! Training Flushing Spaniels the American Way*. New York: Howell Book House, 1992.

Spencer, James B. *Point! Training the All-Seasons Birddog*. New York: Howell Book House, 1995.

Tarrant, Bill. *Training the Hunting Retriever*. New York: Howell Book House, 1991.

Volhard, Jack and Wendy. *The Canine Good Citizen*. New York: Howell Book House, 1994.

General Titles

Haggerty, Captain Arthur J. *How to Get Your Pet Into Show Business*. New York: Howell Book House, 1994.

McLennan, Bardi. *Dogs and Kids, Parenting Tips*. New York: Howell Book House, 1993.

Moran, Patti J. *Pet Sitting for Profit, A Complete Manual for Professional Success*. New York: Howell Book House, 1992.

Scalisi, Danny and Libby Moses. *When Rover Just Won't Do, Over 2,000 Suggestions for Naming Your Dog.* New York: Howell Book House, 1993.

Sife, Wallace, PhD. *The Loss of a Pet.* New York: Howell Book House, 1993.

Wrede, Barbara J. *Civilizing Your Puppy.* Hauppauge, N.Y.: Barron's Educational Series, 1992.

Magazines

The AKC GAZETTE, The Official Journal for the Sport of Purebred Dogs. American Kennel Club, 51 Madison Ave., New York, NY.

Bloodlines Journal. United Kennel Club, 100 E. Kilgore Rd., Kalamazoo, MI.

Dog Fancy. Fancy Publications, 3 Burroughs, Irvine, CA 92718

Dog World. Maclean Hunter Publishing Corp., 29 N. Wacker Dr., Chicago, IL 60606.

Videos

"SIRIUS Puppy Training," by Ian Dunbar, PhD, MRCVS. James & Kenneth Publishers, 2140 Shattuck Ave. #2406, Berkeley, CA 94704. Order from the publisher.

"Training the Companion Dog," from Dr. Dunbar's British TV Series, James & Kenneth Publishers. (See address above).

The American Kennel Club produces videos on every breed of dog, as well as on hunting tests, field trials and other areas of interest to purebred dog owners. For more information, write to AKC/Video Fulfillment, 5580 Centerview Dr., Suite 200, Raleigh, NC 27606.

chapter 13

Resources

Breed Clubs

Every breed recognized by the American Kennel Club has a national (parent) club. National clubs are a great source of information on your breed. You can get the name of the secretary of the club by contacting:

The American Kennel Club
51 Madison Avenue
New York, NY 10010
(212) 696-8200

There are also numerous all-breed, individual breed, obedience, hunting and other special-interest dog clubs across the country. The American Kennel Club can provide you with a geographical list of clubs to find ones in your area. Contact them at the above address.

Registry Organizations

Registry organizations register purebred dogs. The American Kennel Club is the oldest and largest in this country, and currently recognizes over 130 breeds. The United Kennel Club registers some breeds the AKC doesn't (including the American Pit Bull Terrier and the Miniature Fox Terrier) as well as many of the same breeds. The others included here are for your reference; the AKC can provide you with a list of foreign registries.

American Kennel Club
51 Madison Avenue
New York, NY 10010

United Kennel Club (UKC)
100 E. Kilgore Road
Kalamazoo, MI 49001-5598

American Dog Breeders Assn.
P.O. Box 1771
Salt Lake City, UT 84110
(Registers American Pit Bull Terriers)

Canadian Kennel Club
89 Skyway Avenue
Etobicoke, Ontario
Canada M9W 6R4

National Stock Dog Registry
P.O. Box 402
Butler, IN 46721
(Registers working stock dogs)

Orthopedic Foundation for Animals (OFA)
2300 E. Nifong Blvd.
Columbia, MO 65201-3856
(Hip registry)

Activity Clubs

Write to these organizations for information on the
activities they sponsor.

American Kennel Club
51 Madison Avenue
New York, NY 10010
(Conformation Shows, Obedience Trials, Field
Trials and Hunting Tests, Agility, Canine Good

Citizen, Lure Coursing, Herding, Tracking, Earthdog Tests, Coonhunting.)

United Kennel Club
100 E. Kilgore Road
Kalamazoo, MI 49001-5598
(Conformation Shows, Obedience Trials, Agility, Hunting for Various Breeds, Terrier Trials and more.)

North American Flyball Assn.
1342 Jeff St.
Ypsilanti, MI 48198

International Sled Dog Racing Assn.
P.O. Box 446
Norman, ID 83848-0446

North American Working Dog Assn., Inc.
Southeast Kreisgruppe
P.O. Box 833
Brunswick, GA 31521

Trainers

Association of Pet Dog Trainers
P.O. Box 385
Davis, CA 95617
(800) PET–DOGS

American Dog Trainers' Network
161 West 4th St.
New York, NY 10014
(212) 727–7257

National Association of Dog Obedience Instructors
2286 East Steel Rd.
St. Johns, MI 48879

Associations

American Dog Owners Assn.
1654 Columbia Tpk.
Castleton, NY 12033
(Combats anti-dog legislation)

Delta Society
P.O. Box 1080
Renton, WA 98057-1080
(Promotes the human/animal bond through
pet-assisted therapy and other programs)

Dog Writers Assn. of America (DWAA)
Sally Cooper, Secy.
222 Woodchuck Ln.
Harwinton, CT 06791

National Assn. for Search and Rescue (NASAR)
P.O. Box 3709
Fairfax, VA 22038

Therapy Dogs International
6 Hilltop Road
Mendham, NJ 07945